THE POWER OF SELF-KINDNESS

THE POWER OF SELF-KINDNESS

HOW TO TRANSFORM YOUR RELATIONSHIP WITH YOUR INNER CRITIC

HANNAH BRAIME

INDIVIDUATE PRESS

The Power of Self-Kindness: How to Transform Your Relationship With Your Inner Critic.

ISBN: 978-1916059122

Published by Individuate Press

Cover Illustration by Alexander Kharchenko © 123RF.com

Edited by Sandy Draper

CONTENTS

INTRODUCTION

LISTENING TO THE WHISPERS

For as long as I can remember, I've experienced a compelling and convincing voice in my head. This voice would tell me that I wasn't good enough because I got 97 per cent on a test at school but my friend got 98 per cent. If she had done better, I should have done better too. Later, this voice would tell me my career wasn't where it should be, I should be earning more money and that I was a failure. When I thought about leaving a bad relationship, this voice told me I would always be alone and no one else would want me. Whenever I looked in the mirror, this voice pointed out all my flaws and imperfections.

Sometimes this voice was a whisper of a thought. Sometimes it was a roar: *You're a waste of space, the world would be better off without you and your life will never amount to anything.* The exact script changed depending on the situation and the context, but the message was always the same: *You are worthless, you suck at life and it's only a matter of time before people see you for who you really are (and that, so we're crystal clear, is a not-good person).*

Ouch.

I tried many approaches to rein in this destructive background chatter: ignoring it, yelling at it (in my head), telling it to shut up, trying to drown it out with positive affirmations and good vibes, but nothing worked. The louder I yelled, the louder it yelled back. The more I tried to affirm, the more my inner critic told me I was a liar and what I was doing was ridiculous. I was trying to out-yell, out-affirm, and outmanoeuvre my inner critic. I won small battles here and there but, overall, I was losing the war.

Thus far, I'd spent most of my life waiting, placing my hopes on the next big milestone – leaving home, getting into university, graduating, getting a job and so on, thinking then, surely then, I would feel better about myself and this incessant chatter would cease. But I didn't and it didn't.

And then I realized, rather than *waiting* for things to get better, I would have to *do* something about it. I had always been interested in psychology, but my focus shifted to using it to reach greater self-understanding. I began to learn more about my inner critic and how its voice was influencing my life. I also began to understand where my inner critic came from, and how to deal with this out-of-control presence and its, often, 24/7 (unwelcome) running commentary.

During my adventures into the often weird, sometimes wonderful world of personal growth, I came across a school of therapy called "Internal Family Systems" (IFS), whose concepts were the polar opposite of almost everything else I'd heard about the inner critic up to that point.

The IFS approach suggested the inner critic wasn't a gremlin or a monster, but part of our internal dialogue that was fearful, hurting and *trying to keep us safe*. Since none of my previous attempts to shut down my inner critic had worked, I decided to try dealing with my critic as though that were the case and see what happened.

While much of the IFS approach doesn't resonate with me, its insight into my inner critic has transformed the way I approach it. Instead of being combative and angry – trying to match it at its own game – I've learned to look beyond its harsh words and sweeping judgements to question: "What's going on here? What's this really about?" Rather than telling my inner critic to shut up or trying to ignore it, keep calm and carry on, I now pay more attention to it. I also use tools like journaling (something I'll talk about more later in this book) to slow down my interactions with my inner critic and ask it: "What are you afraid of? What do you believe about this situation?"

I used therapy to explore why my inner critic had developed in the way it had and to release some of the scripts I'd been raised with. Scripts my inner critic was clinging to, in the belief that I still needed protecting, but that didn't apply to my life as an adult and ones I no longer needed. For example, if there was a chance someone was upset, angry or disappointed because of something I'd done or said, my inner critic would tell me that it was my job to make them feel better because it was my fault they felt that way. The fact they were unhappy with me was proof that I was a bad person, all my relationships were on tenterhooks, and it was only a matter of time before everyone would leave and I'd end up all alone.

Before, this script would have triggered a knee-jerk response. I would have felt an overwhelming desire to rush in and fix everything – even if that meant overriding my own feelings, experiences, values and needs. Or I would honour them, while experiencing gut-wrenching anxiety and the unshakeable sense that I was doing something wrong. Or I would respond with defensiveness and blame the other person for having feelings (how dare they!) or avoid the situation altogether and feel like the worst person in the world. But when I began treating my inner critic like a valid part of my internal dialogue and extending self-acceptance to all parts of myself, I started slowing down my thoughts and taking the time to ask: *What's the story I'm telling myself about this situation? Are there any other interpretations that I might be overlooking? What's the belief underneath these words? And, outside this belief, what do I know to be true?* Now that I use this more detached, questioning approach, I am less likely to get swept up in my inner critic's panic. Instead, I pause to peel back the layers, strip away the harsh words, and try to understand what's underneath the surface – what's driving my inner critic and what is its *raison d'être*?

This new approach has transformed my life in several ways. I no longer view other people's uncomfortable feelings as something I need to fix: they can have their feelings and I can have mine – both are valid. It's not always comfortable, but I no longer assume it's automatically my fault or a sign that I'm flawed. At the same time, I take greater ownership for my behaviour and decisions, and make amends where necessary, rather than avoiding situations that make me uncomfortable. I'm much better at setting boundaries. I compare myself unfavourably to others less often. I'm also less self-absorbed – and because I'm better able to empathize with myself, I'm better able to empathize with other people. Rather than spending most of my time worrying about what they're thinking of me, I can better understand the world from their perspective. I take more reasonable risks, am open to more opportunities and try more things. Rather than making judgements, I try to keep an open mind. I've found the courage to create and share my thoughts, opinions and ideas through my website, www.becomingwhoyouare.net, and support other writers and artists as a creative coach. I've also learned more about other aspects of my internal world, the other voices present in my internal dialogue, and how I can use them to mediate with and counteract the destructive effects of my inner critic.

And the biggest change? *I trust my ability to handle my inner critic.* I don't need my inner critic to change because I know I can deal with it. While I was trying to drown it out or ignore it, I thought taking this approach would make me feel more powerful and my inner critic less so, fuelled by the new-age idea that what we focus on grows. *Talk to the hand, inner critic.* But really, I was reinforcing the message: *I cannot handle this part of myself (and therefore I cannot handle myself as I actually am),* which only fed my inner-critic's message that I wasn't good enough or acceptable as I am.

Now, I'm no longer waiting for the magical day when I'll wake up to find my inner critic has gone for good. I have an inner critic, sometimes a vocal one, and I'm okay with that. As counterintuitive as it sounds, I've found facing my inner critic head on, being willing to see and accept it for what it is, and showering it with understanding, empathy and compassion, has made it less powerful, less dominant and less of a controlling force in my life.

This way of viewing my inner critic has been the most transformative and has had a profoundly positive impact on my life, and it's the approach I want to share with you. As we'll explore, your inner critic came into existence for a good reason: to keep you in line with the beliefs, rules and scripts you grew up with – also known as "conditioning". Throughout this book, you'll find ideas, tools and resources to help you regain leadership of all parts of yourself and transform your relationship with your inner critic by using acceptance, understanding and your own internal strength.

Personal growth is *personal* and different approaches for dealing with their inner critic work for different people, so I'm not presenting this as a one-size-fits-all solution. Instead, I'm sharing the process that worked for me – turning down the volume on my inner critic and turning up the volume on another part of my internal dialogue, one I call my "inner mentor" (which we'll explore in Part II). However, the most important thing is to find an approach that works for you, so I encourage you to take the ideas that resonate with you and feel free to leave any parts that don't.

It feels important to share right here, in the beginning, that creating and maintaining a harmonious inner world, negotiating with myself and practising self-kindness will be a lifelong journey for me – and perhaps it will be for you too. Like all the important relationships in our lives, our relationship with ourselves requires attention, maintenance and work. It's not something you do once, check off your to-do list, and consider done and dusted. It will probably involve conflict, discomfort, revelations, mistakes and forgiveness, as well as intimacy, belonging, laughter, peace and fulfilment.

When I first became interested in personal growth, my aim was to cure myself of negative thinking and inner conflict. Then, I figured, my life would really begin; I would be free. However, I've discovered I don't need to be free of self-criticism to truly live, nor is it realistic to expect to be free of self-judgement and internal conflict 100 per cent of the time. Just as I sometimes disagree with, feel negatively toward or experience conflict with the people I love and care about, so I experience those things with myself too.

As I've been writing this book, my inner critics have been along for the ride. (Yes, you can have more than one critic, as I'll explain in the next chapter.) Describing one of my inner critics in Part I (the one who is shaming and tells me I'm worthless and undeserving), not for the first time I wondered if I should keep going. A thought chimed in, breaking my writing flow: *What are people going to think of you? You will have zero credibility if you talk about this.* Another critic. But, as I talk about throughout this book, I can't change my critics. I can influence them, but I don't have control over when they speak up or what they say. What I can change, and have control over, is *how I respond to them*. This is what I want to share with you: how you can encourage your inner critics to rise to meet you, learn to negotiate with them for greater internal harmony, and live your life to the full.

I encourage you to start by thinking of your relationship

with yourself as you would any other relationship in your life. It takes work, it's not always easy and you will feel all the feelings – good and bad. But, while other people might come and go, your relationship with yourself is the one constant in your life. For that reason alone, it's the one worth paying the most attention to.

How to Use This Book

This book is divided into two parts, which will guide you through the process of gaining a deeper understanding of your inner critics (and your internal dialogue in general), connecting with and identifying your inner mentor, and finally creating a working partnership between these important parts of your inner world. Along the way, I'll be sharing insights from my personal experience, my work as a life coach and stories from other people's experience of their inner critics.

At the end of each chapter, you'll find some questions for reflection and practical exercises to help you make powerful shifts in your perspective so that you can start to change how you view both your inner critic and yourself. I've also offered suggestions for further reading as you move forward on your personal journey, and these are based on some of my favourite books and resources on this topic.

Part I is all about becoming more aware of, and understanding, your inner critic. You'll learn about the different types of inner critic, how they show up, and learn to identify how they are influencing and affecting your life today. You'll also explore where your critics come from and, in doing so, develop a deeper understanding of why they say the things they say. Then, you'll explore a radical approach to dealing with your inner critics: not by telling them to shut up or calling them names like "jerk" or "gremlin", but by accepting them as parts of yourself (albeit misguided ones) and learning to work with them, rather than against them. With this, you'll look at different ways you can respond to your inner critics that model the respect and understanding you'd like them to show you.

In Part II, you'll discover your inner mentor – another internal voice but one that can help you keep your critics in check and offers a more supportive, constructive, nurturing approach to your daily life. You'll discover different practices and ideas you can use to turn up the volume on your inner mentor and strengthen this invaluable part of your internal dialogue. And in the final chapter, you'll learn how your inner critics can actually be helpful, and how your inner critics and inner mentor can work together to help you be who you want to be, do what you want to do, and create what you want to create in your life.

As you'll see in Part I, you can have more than one kind of inner critic. Since you might usually talk and think about your inner critic in the singular, I've used the singular "inner critic" and plural "inner critics" interchangeably throughout the book, however, it's worth remembering for you the term "inner critic" might refer to more than one kind of critic. In addition, I mention articles, books, and resources I've found insightful or interesting. For brevity, I haven't included links or references in the text but have compiled everything in the Resources at the back of the book.

There are two ways you can use this book. The first is to read it straight through, then go back and revisit the sections that resonate most for you. Alternatively, you can return to the beginning and work through it, one chapter at a time, answering the Questions for Reflection at the end of each chapter as you go. These questions encourage you to turn theory into practice and explore your relationship with your own inner critics and inner mentor. You can also find these questions collected together in the Appendix. Each set of questions builds on the one before, so I invite you to take a break from reading to think about your responses and take a few notes or spend time journaling about them.

Before we start, I want to highlight that this is a self-guided journey, which means you are in charge of how deep you go with your inner-critic work. Please be mindful of your mental health. If your inner critic has been running the show for some time and you find yourself feeling overwhelmed, powerless or worthless frequently, and if you have thoughts involving self-harm, *please seek support*. Being objective about my inner critic hasn't been easy, especially since I spent years absorbing what it told me as truth. When I look back on past situations, I can see how I've made decisions and behaved in alignment with thoughts and beliefs I didn't even realize were coming from my inner critic. As I've redefined my relationship with my critics, I've also found that, at times, addressing my inner critics – their many faces and how they've influenced my life – has felt like too much to unravel on my own. If you have a similar experience at any point on your journey, I encourage you to take care of yourself first. If you sense you might benefit from support in unpacking your inner critic's origins, motivations and manifestations, I recommend enlisting the services of a qualified counsellor for this part of your journey.

As you will see, I mention counselling and therapy several times throughout this book and I do so because the right counsellor or therapist can be an invaluable ally as you redefine your relationship with your inner critic. A good therapist – one who is well-versed in dealing with inner critics and able to mirror a more nurturing, compassionate voice – can help you explore your relationship with your inner critics in a contained, supported environment. Whatever your relationship with your inner critic is like – whether it's something that is an irritation every now and again or something that is affecting your quality of life – the right outside perspective can help you realize things about yourself and your internal world you won't notice alone. I talk more about finding a good therapist and qualities to look for in Chapter 8.

In the next chapters, we'll start by looking at a different way of viewing yourself and your inner critic. You'll learn more about your internal dialogue and how it's much larger than just your inner critic (even if that's all you can hear right now), and you'll come to understand your inner critic on a deeper level, paving the way for a more enriching and accepting relationship with yourself.

This self-exploration has changed my life for the better and I hope it will do the same for you too.

Stay kind to yourself,

Hannah

P.S. Would you like a free video class on self-kindness to

complement your journey as you transform your relationship with your inner critic and yourself? Simply go to http://selfkindness.becomingwhoyouare.net and enter your email to access to the class. When you register, you'll also get more free workbooks, video classes and more tools for cultivating courage, compassion, and creativity in the Becoming Who You Are Library (I will never, ever share your email and you are free to unsubscribe at any time).

1

INTRODUCING YOUR INNER CRITICS

"Of all the judgments we pass in life, none is more important than the judgment we pass on ourselves."

—Nathaniel Branden

1

YOU CONTAIN MULTITUDES

Before diving in, let's start by looking at some of the different ways our inner critics can manifest and where they fit within the landscape of our internal dialogue.

When I wind back the tape on my long journey toward transforming my relationship with my inner critic, I can see the first big turning point was discovering the ideas that I'll be sharing with you in this chapter.

Up to that point – even when I didn't believe what my inner critic was saying – I would hear its voice in my head saying horrible things about me, my life and my future, and think there must be something wrong with me, that I was somehow broken or flawed for hearing this voice. After all, if I was thinking these things, and being affected by them, was it a sign that I was messed up, maybe even irredeemable? This way of thinking fit with the beliefs I was carrying from years before – and they were sticky. But even though I was in pain, and wanted to stop the internal bullying, trying to do so through brute force just made my inner critic louder and the pain even worse. It was only when I learned to reframe how I viewed myself – and how my inner critic fit into the context of my wider self – that my relationship with its negative voice (and my thoughts and feelings overall) began to change for the better. These ideas might sound wacky if you're new to them. Even so, stick with me because this concept could change how you relate to yourself for good.

In this chapter I want to introduce an idea that is foundational for redefining your relationship with your inner critic and changing the way you view yourself. You'll discover that, rather than having a personality in the singular, you have multiple internal voices – each with a different viewpoint, different needs and different strategies for getting what they want (including the inner critic). Accepting and understanding these different parts of your inner world is key to transforming your relationship with your inner critic. This journey starts with becoming more aware of what these different voices are saying and understanding their beliefs, needs and desires. In this chapter, you'll learn more about some key parts of your internal dialogue and how to become more aware of how they interact.

The Many Faces of You and Me

The problem is we tend to think of ourselves in the singular. I am "me" and you are "you". But who are you? Beyond the objective facts, this can be a tricky question to answer.

For me, when it comes to the essence of who I am, there is lots to say. I have been told that I have a calm demeanour, but I feel feelings intensely and can also get jumping up-and-down excited about tiny things. I yearn for both adventure and stability. I am capable of being both mature and childish. I am pragmatic when it comes to some areas of life and deeply impractical when it comes to others. In the words of Walt Whitman, "I am large, I contain multitudes."

I'm guessing if you looked at your own decisions, needs, desires and ambitions, you too would find similar contradictions. Keep reading and you'll start to get a sense of these different voices, why your inner critic is so vocal, why it's possible to be at war with yourself and, most importantly, how to make a peace treaty with yourself so you can really start thriving.

One theory of personality is that we are made up of multiple sub-personalities or "parts", each with their own mini-personality, needs, desires and motivations. As a society, we tend to think of hearing voices in our heads as a sign of madness. The truth, however, is that we all have an internal dialogue in our heads which provides a running commentary on what's happening in the moment, creating thoughts, reminding us of memories, evoking feelings and more. The aspects of myself I described above, and many more, might seem like contradictions, but they represent different parts of my personality. My inner critic is one of these parts.

Here's an example of how these different voices can interact and influence us:

Imagine your alarm goes off first thing in the morning. You wake up, turn off the alarm (or, if you're like me, snooze it). Then, you might notice the thought, *I should really get up and go to the gym*, immediately followed by another thought: *But I'm tired and it's still dark outside, I want to stay in bed*. In this scenario, the first part is rooting for you to exercise, while the second part isn't so convinced – that part wants to stay comfy and cosy in bed. On a micro level, these two parts have competing desires and will do their best to persuade you that their way is the right way. Which part wins depends on which part you let dominate.

As psychologist and Internal Family Systems psychotherapist Jay Earley explains in his essay for *The Self-Acceptance Project*:

> "It's helpful to think of the parts like little people inside us with their own motivations and fears . . . if you treat your parts as if they are little people you can talk to, the parts respond in a very positive way."

Recognizing Your Internal Dialogue

I'll explain more about how viewing yourself as the sum of multiple parts can help you redefine your relationship with your inner critic later. For now, let's look at how to become more aware of your internal dialogue, and build a picture of the different parts and voices that exist for you.

The daily chatter that runs through your head reveals more about your beliefs and internal stories than you might realize. Listen to your thoughts and pay particular attention to the language you use toward yourself. Initially, and especially if you have a very vocal inner critic, you might find it easier to start by identifying the more negative elements of your internal dialogue.

Language to watch out for related to your inner critic includes:

- Shoulds – "I should do ABC", "I should have done XYZ", "I should be more . . .", "I should be less . . ."
- "When I have [*insert dream, goal or desire*], then I'll be happy."
- Criticism disproportionate to the current situation.
- Name-calling – "I'm such a failure."
- Scarcity-based language – "I'm not [*insert good, smart, pretty, organized, etc.*] enough."
- Talking yourself out of opportunities.
- Comparing yourself to other people, as a way of beating yourself up rather than inspiring yourself.
- Using absolutes – "I *never* get it right," "I *always* screw up," "*Everyone* will think I'm an idiot," "I'll *always* be alone."

I'd also encourage you to notice the times when you reassure yourself, encourage yourself, give yourself a pep talk, convince yourself into or out of doing something with compassion, and acknowledge your wins and successes. Finally, pay attention to how these other voices interact with your inner critic, if they do. Do they tell it to shut up? Do they crumble and acquiesce? Do they offer a firm and fair counter-perspective?

For now, simply notice where your inner critic is present in your internal dialogue and where self-compassion is more dominant. Again, you don't need to do anything about this, at this stage you're just building awareness.

Before we move on to exploring the inner critic in more

depth, let's take a few moments to explore some of the other major characters you might discover in your internal dialogue. As we'll explore later in this book, transforming your relationship isn't about stamping out your inner critic, but learning to create balance and harmony among all the parts of your internal dialogue (rather than the inner critic drowning them out). As I mentioned in the Introduction, your relationship with yourself is deeply personal, so I offer these not as a framework with which to view yourself, but as a lens through which you can better understand your inner world, and how your thoughts and feelings affect how you interact with your outer world.

Inner Critics

The next chapter is all about our hard-working inner critics, but I am including them here as they are significant as you'll learn shortly.

Inner Mentor

Our inner mentors are the wise, compassionate parts of ourselves that act as a mediator/protector against the inner critic and its potential for causing harm. Again, since we will cover the inner mentor in more depth in Part II, I will only mention it here.

Inner Child

The inner child is a popular concept in self-help psychology and refers to the part of yourself that is child-like, whatever your actual age. This is the part of you that feels elated while bouncing on a trampoline, dissolves into an uncontrollable fit of giggles after a friend makes a silly joke or disappears down a rabbit hole of adorable and funny cat videos online (or that's my inner child, anyway). At its best, this part of ourselves can be spontaneous, present, playful and fun-loving. But when dominant in challenging situations, or at odds with our inner critics, it might also leave us feeling powerless, helpless and psychologically shrunken in the face of setbacks, challenges and difficult behaviour from others, regardless of how much power and agency we actually have. Our inner child is a part that is directly polarized with our inner critics (this is something we'll discuss in more depth later in this book). That means the critic knows exactly how to provoke it and push its buttons. When you react to an onslaught from your inner critic – by making yourself small, hiding or shrinking – it is usually a sign that your inner child is in the driving seat, dominating your reaction.

True Self/Aware Ego

Your true self (also called the "Aware Ego") is an internal part that differs from the others because it is more of a detached observer, without judgement and without an agenda. The true self, or Aware Ego, is the part that says, *Oh, this is my inner critic talking and that is my inner child feeling hurt*. You'll know when your true self is speaking up because it doesn't come with the same emotional weight as the inner critic or inner child. While your inner child might feel persecuted and victimized by your inner critic, or your inner mentor might give you encouragement or offer guidance to put the critic in its place (or you might experience yet another part of your dialogue getting frustrated and piping up, *That critic . . . what a jerk!*), the true self notices what is. Your true self is the part of you that can hold all of your apparent contradictions and opposing parts and give them all space and a seat at the table.

While I believe we all have a true self, the way we experience it will be different for all of us. Psychologists Hal and Sidra Stone, in their book *Embracing the Inner Critic*, describe the Aware Ego as being more of a process than a dominant "self". For me, this aspect of myself is akin to the part of my inner life that dominates (or, at least, ideally dominates) during meditation, when I practice noticing my thoughts and feelings, then dropping them. I mention the true self/Aware Ego here because this practise of noticing can be invaluable in removing some of the emotional weight from your interactions with your inner critic and righting your internal balance of power.

Summary

In this chapter, we've explored a different way of thinking about and relating to ourselves – one that until now might be new and unfamiliar. You've discovered we all have a rich and varied internal dialogue and begun the process of identifying the different parts of your internal dialogue by learning more about some key "characters" that influence your internal world and can help you transform your relationship with your inner critic.

In the next chapter, we'll dive deeper into the inner critic, learning more about how it operates and exploring why it does what it does – a key understanding that will help you to begin to transform your relationship with it and create greater internal harmony.

Questions for Reflection

1. *Can you start to pair parts of your self-dialogue with parts of your personality? Alongside your inner critic, do you also recognize an inner child, inner mentor, and true self/Aware Ego?*
2. *Over the next week, dedicate a page in your journal, or make a note on your phone, titled "Internal Dialogue". Whenever you become conscious of a particular thought about yourself running through your head, make a note of it. You might also find it helpful to make time for reflection at the end of each day and note down any self-talk that's been prominent over the last 24 hours. At the end of the week, review what you've written. Do you notice any patterns in your self-talk? Are there certain phrases or messages that come up more frequently than others?*
3. *How have you dealt with your inner critic so far? What has worked? And what hasn't? After reading this chapter, how do you plan to approach your inner critic from here?*
4. *If you were 5 per cent more empathic with all parts of yourself over the next week, what would you do differently?*

2

THE MANY VOICES OF THE INNER CRITIC

Even if you call it by a different name, you need no introduction to your inner critic. This is the voice – or voices – who can take you down a peg or two (or several) with one well-aimed blow. Our inner critic seems to know exactly what to say and when to say it for maximum effect. It's a master of the psychological KO, leaving us feeling like the smallest, most flawed, most disempowered version of ourselves.

> *You're not clever enough to do that.*
>
> *Who would want to read anything you write?*
>
> *Of course he wouldn't want to date you, look at your life.*
>
> *She's way prettier than you'll ever be.*
>
> *There's no point in even trying, everyone already thinks you're a joke.*

Countless people have written about the inner critic, using terms like "gremlin" or "monster", advising readers to just ignore their inner critic or tell it to shut up and get lost. Perhaps, like me, you've tried this approach and found it doesn't work. As the Irish playwright George Bernard Shaw has been quoted as saying, "Never wrestle with pigs. You both get dirty and the pig likes it." So in this chapter, you'll learn why and discover a different, perhaps counterintuitive, way of dealing with your inner critic that can help you develop a more harmonious relationship with this important and impactful part of your internal dialogue.

Once I began to look at my internal dialogue as a sum of multiple parts, rather than a single entity, I noticed the same concept applied to my inner critic too. My inner critic came in different flavours, presented in different ways in different situations and each one had a different effect on my life.

The first step toward transforming your relationship with your inner critic involves facing it head on and examining how it shows up in your life. In this chapter, I'll share some different types of inner critic you might encounter, their effects and why – contrary to popular belief – your inner critic is not the gremlin you might have believed it to be. Along the way, I'll also share ideas that will encourage you to reflect on your own inner critic and develop a deeper understanding of this part of your internal dialogue. As we'll explore in this chapter, inner critics come in all shapes and sizes. You might identify one of the critics I describe below, or you might identify a smorgasbord (lucky you!). While you read this chapter, think about which critics are most present for you.

As I mentioned in the previous chapter, we all have

thoughts running through our head all day long. As you start paying attention to these thoughts, you will notice they belong to different aspects or parts of yourself. This becomes particularly apparent in situations that involve a degree of internal negotiation. Returning to the scenario I described in Chapter 1, the part that is responsible for thoughts like, *Come on, stay in bed. You don't need to go to the gym today . . .* differs from the part behind the thought, *Yes, you do. You've said this every morning for the last three days and you'll regret it if you let this inactive streak continue. It's time to get up and go.* In an ideal world, these internal parts are benevolent, open to negotiation and work together to support our best selves.

But then there's the inner critic . . .

If your internal dialogue was at a party, your inner critic would be *that* person going from group to group, spreading gossip, creating rumours and causing social mayhem, all while making loud comments about how much this party sucks and what a crappy host you are. Instead of constructive motivation like the firm but fair voice I mentioned above, your critic will meet your morning resistance with something like, *Of course you're finding it hard to get up and go to the gym; you're a lazy slob,* or *What the hell is wrong with you? No one else finds it this hard to get up in the morning,* or *There's no point in going to the gym, everyone else there is in much better shape than you and you look like an idiot next to them.* No wonder we think of the inner critic as a jerk . . . As difficult as it can be to face your critics – internal and external – changing your relationship with them starts with awareness and getting to know them better.

The Many Faces of the Inner Critics

Most, if not all, of us have several critical voices in our heads, each with a different *modus operandi*. Even though the situations in which they show up – and how they try to manipulate our behaviour – are different they all aim to keep certain aspects of our personality hidden away from the outside world.

Jay Earley, whom I quoted earlier in this book, and psychotherapist Bonnie Weiss outline seven types of inner critic. Look at the following list and notice which kinds of inner critic are present for you:

- **The perfectionist:** Sets high, usually unobtainable, standards and struggles to call things completed or finished.
- **The underminer:** Undermines your self-confidence and abilities so you stay small and don't take risks.
- **The guilt-tripper:** Criticizes you for past wrong-doings and lives by the standards set by your family, community or culture.
- **The molder:** Tries to get you to fit a certain shape or standard set by your family, community or culture, and fears showing your true self will lead to rejection and abandonment.
- **The destroyer:** Attacks your self-worth, says you are inherently flawed and undeserving of basic respect and understanding.
- **The taskmaster:** Pushes you to keep going and fears if you stop, you will become lazy or other people will judge you as a failure (I write about

my own experiences with my inner taskmaster later).

- **The inner controller:** Tries to control your impulses around things like eating, drinking, spending and sex – often resorting to harsh tactics to do so (you might recognize this inner critic in the gym scenario I described earlier in this chapter).

As you read this list, you might have an inkling which inner critic is loudest for you. Perhaps, like me, you experience more than one. Depending on which kinds of inner critic you experience, you'll also notice a range of behaviours and thought patterns from them, some of which overlap and combine. These include:

- **Name-calling**: "Idiot!"
- **Labelling**: "You're lazy."
- **Should and musts (in a positive or negative context)**: "You *should* do X because otherwise, people will judge you," "You *must* not say that – they'll think you're crazy!"
- **Generalizations**: "You're *always* so awkward," "You *never* get it right."
- **Black-and-white thinking**: Situations are fantastic or terrible with no in-between. Something is impossible or you should be able to do it perfectly first time. If you are not totally wonderful, you are utterly useless
- **A fixed mindset:** Things are the way they are right now, with no hope for change or growth in the future: "You will always be terrible at this."
- **The generalized "other" and "everyone"**:

> "*Everyone* will think you're ridiculous," "What will *other people* say?!"

The Effects of the Inner Critics

Although, as I'll explain in the following pages, your inner critic believes it is working in your best interests, I'm guessing you're already aware of how its barrage of criticism, hurtful comments and verbal abuse has a negative effect on your life. Looking back on times when my inner critic has been an uncontrollable and unpredictable presence in my life, I recognize a number self-sabotaging behaviours and unwanted patterns in myself, which have been frustrating, hurtful and evoked shame – not to mention damaged my relationships with other people. You might already know well some of the negative effects caused by your inner critic and you might also experience negative effects where you haven't yet joined the dots – perhaps attributing them to being "just the way you are". These effects might be internal, affecting how you feel about and perceive yourself, and external, affecting how you show up in the world.

On a physiological level, our reactions to our inner critics can be divided into four general categories: fight, flight, freeze and submit. If you *fight*, you might find that not only do you have a vocal inner critic, but you also criticize yourself for having an inner critic. If you notice you tend to deal with an inner-critic onslaught with escapism and numbing (such as eating or drinking to excess), you likely fall into the *flight* category. If, on the other hand, your inner critic leaves you feeling paralysed and you find yourself ruminating on its judgements and all the ways it says you're not good enough, your go-to reaction is probably *freeze*. Finally if your default response is to *submit*, you tend to accept what your critic says unquestioningly and internalize their criticisms of you as the truth.

You might also experience a combination of two or more of these responses. When I look back on times my inner critic has been in control and how I responded on a physiological level, I can see how it has affected my life and I've listed some of these below. It's important to note this is not an exhaustive list and my experience of my inner critics might differ to your experience with yours: how the inner critics can affect you on an individual level is unique and deeply personal to you.

Inaction

Although I am a hard worker and capable of being intensely productive, inaction – particularly around projects or activities that are meaningful to me – is something I have to be especially mindful of. This is due to my vocal perfectionist inner critic. You'll know if you're also on team perfection because you might have thoughts like: *There's no point in starting, you'll only screw it up at some point.* You might also feel such daunting pressure to do well with the task or project you're undertaking that you avoid it until the last moment, or even completely. During school and university, I would procrastinate when I should have been preparing for important exams, then cram, cram, cram the night before and on the morning itself. At the root of this behaviour, I was giving myself an out. If I did badly, it was due to last-minute cramming, not because I wasn't good enough (which was what my inner critic was telling me). Although this approach mostly worked out better than it should have, it was stressful and is not one I recommend. The pressure – avoidance – scapegoat cycle is common. Even just noticing it can change your response and transform the way you approach meaningful projects and activities.

These days, I find this cycle shows up differently and manifests more as ideas that my critic shuts down before I even get started. Not all these ideas are good, but my inner critic is indiscriminate; if it's come from me it will be terrible. I counteract this internal chatter by taking the pressure off and remembering my personal aim in life is to create an overall body of work, rather than one project that will define my contribution to the world. With this in mind, I also approach new projects by taking the time to experiment, play around and see what comes out of this process. Once I need to decide whether to commit, I usually have enough evidence that this thing has wings, or it's clear it needs a little more thought and work before I'm ready to move to the next step.

Coping Mechanisms

Self-soothing is a skill I've learned during adulthood thanks mostly to therapy, self-reflection and practice. Before learning these tools, I would deal with the pain and shame provoked by my inner critics by resorting to coping mechanisms. Work, food, alcohol, buying things and zoning out in front of the Internet have all been coping mechanisms for me in the past. Like all coping mechanisms, these things would make me feel better in the moment but lead to greater self-criticism and turbulence in the long term. If you notice a pattern of feeling bad about yourself, or aspects of your life, and turning to a particular activity to feel better – only to feel worse afterwards (or experience negative effects as a result) – this might be something to explore further as you embark on transforming your relationship with your inner critic. I talk about coping mechanisms more in my book *From Coping to Thriving: How to Turn Self-Care into a Way of Life.*

Lack of Self-acceptance

Each of the seven types of critic I describe in this chapter are rooted in a lack of self-acceptance. For example, if you have a strong inner molder, you might struggle to accept the ways in which you don't conform to the values and standards set by the people around you. If you experience a vocal guilt-tripper, you might find it hard to accept your shadow side – the parts of yourself capable of wrong-doing – and/or things you have done in the past.

One of the tricky things about lacking self-acceptance is that it is rarely as obvious as thinking, *I don't accept myself* and rather manifests as more subtle signs – for example, dismissing your feelings to avoid conflict, internally or with others. I can't count the number of times I've felt hurt, angry or upset by something someone has said or done, only to tell myself it isn't a big deal, it doesn't matter and I'm overreacting, as believing this is more comfortable than taking ownership of my feelings. As I learnt more about my inner critics, I realized that even though I wasn't explicitly thinking, *I don't accept my feelings or my experience,* that was the underlying message behind those thoughts. And this lack of self-acceptance was happening for a reason: if I were to take ownership for my feelings and experiences, I might end up having to face up to something uncomfortable within myself, like unhelpful beliefs or attitudes I'm taking out on the other person, and potentially prove my inner critic right – I am a horrible person. Or, I might have to raise the issue with the person concerned, which is an equally scary prospect as they might be displeased or upset and reinforce my inner critic's message – I am unlovable. In doing this, however, I invalidate my own feelings and disown my experience, missing out on the opportunity for greater self-awareness and emotional maturity, or to advocate for my own preferences and needs within a relationship.

One practice I've found most useful for accepting myself – *all* of myself – is journaling, and I invite you to try this too. The act of writing can slow down your thoughts, gives you a safe space to express your feelings and act as a kind of sounding board. My journal won't tell me I'm silly, wrong or shouldn't be writing what I'm writing – and neither will yours. Translating the thoughts and feelings in your head into words on a page will also help you to view them with more emotional distance and see the situation from a different perspective. I will share more journaling practices you can use to heal your relationship with your inner critic later in the book.

Lower Feelings of Self-worth

This effect is self-evident, and it's why the process I'll share in Part II on the inner mentor is so important. If you had someone following you around all day, criticizing all the things they thought you were doing wrong using belligerent and unnecessarily harsh language, reminding you of things that, in their opinion, you've done wrong in the past, and telling you about all the ways people are judging you and so on, you'd feel worn down pretty quickly. What you think about yourself matters and it shapes your stories about yourself. If you're shining a spotlight on the bad or negative at the expense of recognizing the good, this will impact how you see yourself as a person and undermine your feelings of self-worth.

To counteract this tendency within myself, I've done a lot of work around identifying and focusing on my strengths, using tools like journaling to practise identifying and altering negative thought patterns, and adopting mantras and reminders for my daily life, such as one of my favourites, "Assume the best." I'll share more about this in the following pages.

Staying Small and Avoiding Reasonable Risks

At the root of my inner critics' harsh words is a desire to stay small, out of sight, and therefore out of the line of fire of judgement and rejection. Staying small can manifest in many ways, big and small, from which jobs you take and whether you give yourself the opportunity to explore personal dreams and ambitions, to the smaller but significant ways in which you allow yourself to express your individuality – for example how you dress. However, I've found most of the meaningful and fulfilling things I've done and want to do with my life carry some degree of reasonable risk and vulnerability, and this desire to stay small has, at times, stalled my natural process of exploring and developing who I am. This is one of the most insidious effects of the inner critics. I didn't even notice I was doing it until I started to explore how my inner critics were influencing my life. I then realized that I would avoid applying for jobs or going for certain opportunities because I would listen to the voice that popped up saying,

There's no point, everyone else will have much more experience than you. When I experience this voice now, I remind myself of times in the past when I've felt the fear and done it anyway, the times I knew it was a long shot and carried on, and that I have never regretted doing so. As afraid as this part of me is of failure, I've found I carry much less heartbreak about a situation or opportunity if I know I've tried – whatever the outcome – than if I let fear stop me from raising my hand and giving it a go.

Stress, Depression and Anxiety

As Kristen Neff explains in an article on her website, self-compassion.org, self-criticism can cause chronic stress because when we experience an inner-critic onslaught, we are not just engaging in an attack but we are also the ones being attacked – all at the same time. Just as hearing criticism in real life can send your heart racing and put you into fight-or-flight mode, you can have the same response when you are on the receiving end of internal criticism too. This can lead to depression and anxiety over the long term and cause all kinds of stress-related physical health issues. Struggling with overzealous inner critics isn't just a question of feeling dissatisfied with life, it can have a tangible impact on your mental and physical wellbeing.

Relationship Struggles

"You can only love someone else as much as you love yourself" might be a cliché, but like most others, it comes with a strong element of truth. My relationships have been far more fulfilling (and much happier) since I started paying more attention to my relationship with myself. When I didn't feel I was worthy of love and acceptance, I could show those things, but struggled to accept them in return – which meant I often ended up in tangled relationships with people who would treat me the way I thought I deserved to be treated (i.e. not good). Deep down, I believed my friends and boyfriends didn't know who I was, and that they were misguided in their love for me. I assumed too much responsibility for the health and stability of my relationships and believed if the other person wasn't happy, it must be my fault somehow. This undermined my relationships and led to self-sabotaging behaviours and feelings of isolation (which further reinforced the belief I was unlovable).

Many of the effects I've just mentioned create a catch-22 situation. I criticize myself, my self-criticism leads me to change my behaviour, then I start criticizing myself for that change. For example, if I knew I was procrastinating on an important project because of my perfectionist critic, I would then criticize myself for procrastinating, and so creating a vicious cycle of layers self-criticism on self-criticism (I call this the "spiral of self-recrimination", and we'll explore this in more detail in Chapter 5). The same applies to the other effects listed earlier in this chapter, and I've also found these effects can interact. When I've struggled with self-acceptance in relation to past wrongdoings, I have been more likely to avoid making amends because I wanted to avoid the discomfort that comes with thinking about the situation altogether – and this led to inaction and relationship struggles.

Ironically, this is one way that our inner critic can affect the way we show up around other people. When we're in our own heads and focused on what an awful person we are, we're less emotionally available to, and engaged with, the people around us. When we're busy worrying about what other people think of us all the time, we become more self-absorbed because we're making the interaction all about us and whether the other person likes us – ruminating on whether what we just said was stupid and other things that take us into our heads and out of the present moment. As important as addressing your relationship with yourself and your inner critic is for your own internal wellbeing, it's just as important for your relationships too.

What Do Other People's Critics Say?

I asked readers of my website, *Becoming Who You Are* (www.becomingwhoyouare.net), to share the times when their inner critics became vocal. Here are some of their responses:

> "My father always told me to think of others first. Well, somehow, I took it to an extreme and put myself last. I didn't listen to how I felt and escaped into alcoholism. Feeling never good enough, never smart enough. Always trying to 'shine' for someone else."
>
> —Sherrill
>
> "My inner critic says, I'm not good enough at my job. My job isn't even a real job to begin with and I don't make enough money. My value as a person is directly proportional to how hard I work and how much I earn and it's never enough."
>
> —Sebastian
>
> "When I'm preparing for a job interview is when I find

myself self-attacking the worst. I start catastrophizing and tell myself 'I'm going to choke,' 'There are other people more qualified/experienced/skilled than me,' and 'I'm wasting their time even showing up."

—Tom

"I struggle with stress and anxiety – particularly in relation to my teenage children. I can sometimes be overwhelmed by feelings that I'm failing as a mother, or by feelings of profound sadness and worry for their short-term and long-term future."

—Cynthia

"I have experienced a lot of doubt about my relationships: feeling like a burden; feeling like people are putting up with me; feeling like I don't deserve support. I realize now that this is not at all the case and that I have a lot to offer, but it's been a journey getting here and I have to keep on top of it. I'm still working through a lot of core beliefs."

—Lucy

As I mentioned above, this list of the ways in which our inner critics can affect our lives isn't exhaustive. As you become more familiar with your inner critics, you will no doubt become more aware of the ways in which they are influencing your life. So how can you start to change these patterns of thought and behaviour? The first step is to understand what your inner critics are trying to do for you.

I've already mentioned that your inner critic is working for (what it believes to be) your own good. Perhaps that's hard to believe after years of internal conflict and inner-critic abuse, but once you can understand why your critic does what it does, you'll be better placed to teach it how to be more constructive.

It might feel like your inner critic is the loudest, meanest and most powerful of all your inner parts, but it's important to remember that it is just one of the many voices that make up your internal dialogue. It's the one that might sometimes (or often) shout louder than the rest, drowning out thoughts that are kinder and more constructive, but its power is just bluster. At the end of the day, it is just another voice – just like the one that gently reminds you you're tired and hungry so you're not feeling 100 per cent, or the one that urges you to choose cake over fruit for dessert, or the one that chimes in saying it is time to stop Netflix and go to bed. It's also like the calm voice of integrity that reassures you after making an uncomfortable decision that, yes, you have done the right thing, or after making a mistake that, hey, this would be a good way to make amends here. Like these voices, the inner critic has a purpose – to keep you in line with the scripts and beliefs it thinks are important for you to live by.

That's not to say the inner critic doesn't have a very real and negative effect on your life. I know first-hand, just how paralysing, devastating and demoralising our inner critics can be. I've spoken to myself in a way I wouldn't dream of speaking to other people and can be far harsher and more critical of my own actions than those of people I intensely dislike. I know I'm not alone with this. At the same time, your inner critic is just a part of you; it's not in control of you and it doesn't define you as a person. While cultivating a more constructive relationship with my inner critic has taken time (and is a process that continues to this day), it started by realizing that my critic only has as much power as I give it.

I'll repeat that: *Your inner critic only has as much power as you give it.* If you've experienced years of self-attack, this might not ring true, but it is. As a first step, I invite you to at least be open to the possibility that *you* have the power, not your inner critic, and you can redefine your relationship with this part of your internal dialogue.

It's time to step up, take back the reins and be your own leader.

Your Inner Critic Is Not a Gremlin or a Monster

One of the biggest shifts that has helped me change the way I related to my inner critic came from thinking about real-life relationships. I imagined my inner critic was a toddler that had developed the verbal acuity of adults: it felt strong, even overwhelming, feelings and didn't know how to regulate or express them properly (although it could deliver some sophisticated and well-aimed barbs when it wanted to). Just like a toddler, punishing it, or ignoring its behaviour, didn't feel like a good approach. Equally, I don't like it when someone calls me names or tells me to shut up, so why would I expect that to work with my inner critics? If someone is doing this to me, is it going to help if I call them names and tell them to shut up back? No! It's just going to make things worse and escalate the situation. Taking this perspective helped me realize: *I won't change my relationship with my inner critics by descending to their level.* Instead, I'd much rather invite my critics to rise to meet me and model what the right way to interact looks like.

Let's start with the foundation of all good relationships: *respect*. Much conventional advice about how to deal with the inner critic says you need to learn to ignore it, tell it to shut up, or call it names like gremlin, demon or monster. Perhaps you've tried this, and it hasn't worked. Perhaps it works to a degree but talking to a part of yourself like this doesn't quite sit right with you. If this is the case that's for a good reason. This is something we'll explore further in the next chapter; for now, I want to introduce the idea that your inner critic isn't the monster it might appear to be.

Whatever form your inner critic takes (and whatever the specifics of what it says) its overarching purpose is to keep you in line with your "rules for living". Part of its job is to sound the alarm whenever there's a chance you might do something that contravenes these rules and stop you in your tracks before you break them. When you look at the inner critic in this context – that it's trying to keep you in check with the rules you developed to survive – you can see its purpose from a different angle altogether.

Even when it leaves us feeling miserable, the inner critic is trying to protect us. It might not be going about it in the most constructive or helpful way, the rules its upholding might be outdated, and it is almost certainly working to scripts that are no longer helpful, but its modus operandi is self-protection. As I've become more aware of my thoughts, feelings and beliefs, I've discovered that most of my fears and hang-ups come back to two roots: the fear of not being good enough and the fear of being unlovable. The inner critic's fears and hang-ups are no different.

> "In considering where the Inner Critic came from, always keep in mind that the Inner Critic's original function is to spare us shame and pain."
>
> —Hal and Sidra Stone, *Embracing the Inner Critic*

This is why my inner critic is most likely to show up when I'm doing something that takes me outside my comfort zone. Like the time I interviewed for a job I wanted and was still awake at 2 a.m. the morning after, deconstructing everything I should have said and second-guessing myself. Or the time I got my first writing client and avoided their emails for days, paralysed with fear about what would happen if they didn't like my work. Or the countless times I've been in a social situation yet haven't felt able to speak up for fear of people judging me (there's that habit of assuming the worst I mentioned earlier). These are just some of the (many) examples of how my inner critic has shaped the way I respond to situations outside my comfort zone. I'm sure you can think of your own. Going for a promotion, asking someone out, moving to (or even visiting) a new place, trying that new hobby you've always wanted to try; whether the situation is seemingly trivial or life-changing, your inner critic is always there trying to keep you in your safe zone and deter you from doing anything that feels risky, leaves you vulnerable or breaks your internalized rules for life.

"Usually there is some valid concern or point in there, or it's trying to protect me. For example, if my inner critical voice criticizes my work life or earnings, maybe that means there is a part of me that feels concerned about my future financial security. If you ignore the inner critic it always comes back, but if you can hear the real concerns in there and strip out the self-criticisms and judgements, there can be valuable insights."

—Sebastian

So, contrary to popular belief, the inner critic is not a gremlin, or some irrevocably damaged little devil sitting on your shoulder, as you make our way through life. Whether or not you like it, it's a part of you. And, if you want to build a more respectful relationship with your inner critic, that starts with trying to understand and empathize with it. This is what we'll cover in the next chapter.

Summary

In this chapter, we've explored what the inner critic is, the different kinds of critic, how they show up and some of their effects. We've also looked at a different way to think about the inner critic: as a part of us that believes it is doing the right thing by keeping us aligned with the beliefs and scripts we've internalized during our lives – a part that is fearful of breaking the status quo, rejection and abandonment. By now, you hopefully have a better understanding of how your inner critic shows up and how it's impacting your life.

In the next chapter, we'll continue our journey into deepening your understanding of the inner critic by looking in more detail at where it comes from and why it does what it does.

Questions for Reflection

1. *Which of the inner-critic types I mention in this chapter do you recognize in your own internal dialogue? When do they most often show up? Which critic has the biggest impact on your life?*
2. *Which of the inner-critic behaviours and manifestations do you experience most frequently?*
3. *What kind of language do your inner critics use? What are their catchphrases and favourite vocabulary? Are they sarcastic? Frustrated? Spiteful? Bitter? Angry?*
4. *How does your inner critic affect your life? If you have more than one, can you link specific effects to the specific types of inner critics you identified above?*

3

WHERE DO OUR INNER CRITICS COME FROM?

As I dug deeper into my inner critics – their messages and the kinds of things they said – I realized that, contrary to what I had previously believed, my inner critic wasn't just this random voice that had taken up residence in my head. It wasn't a sign I was broken. When I re-read journal entries dominated by or written about my inner critic – or when I heard myself say out loud to a close friend, my partner, or therapist something my inner critic was saying – I realized I sounded like my mother. In fact, one of my inner critics is a replica of my mother, quoting things she said verbatim and carrying the same beliefs, values and fears of what other people will think. This critic is the first to pop up whenever I do (or think of doing) something I imagine my mother would have disapproved of, disagreed with or would have felt threatened by. Even though I don't have a close relationship with my mother as an adult, I still experience the internalized version of her voice. Absorbing my mother's opinions and beliefs was necessary when I was younger. It played the vital role of trying to keep me loved and accepted by someone I depended on for survival. And while I can use the boundary of distance to redefine my relationship with my mother in real life, doing so with the mother in my head has been much harder.

Having explored the different inner critics, and some of the ways they can show up and affect our lives, in this chapter we will dive further into understanding our inner critics and take a deeper look at where they come from and what makes them tick. As you already know, your inner critic exists to keep you in line – making choices and taking actions that (it believes) will keep you safe and sticking to "the script". In this chapter, you'll learn more about how your inner critic operates so you're more aware of when and how it affects your life. With this awareness, you can start to consciously and compassionately encourage it to be more constructive.

Some people don't believe that knowing the origins of critics is important – the only thing that matters is how you deal with them in the present – but this approach doesn't reflect my experience. I've found becoming aware of my critics' origins and intentions has helped me understand them better, depersonalize their messages and get some emotional distance from the things they say. It has also helped me listen to my critics with more objectivity, noticing what they are saying and how they are behaving, without becoming involved in their stories or believing their words as truth. Understanding your thought patterns isn't usually enough to change them (you'll find tangible steps you can take to do that in later chapters), but it is important as part of understanding why the inner critic does what it does, and why ignoring it and/or name-calling doesn't work.

The Genesis of Our Inner Critics

As I got to know my critics in more depth, I could see why they developed and how, even though it was wreaking psychological havoc in my life, my "inner mother" critic existed for a good reason: to protect me. By internalizing my mother's values, her views and her voice as my most vocal inner critic, I could try to avoid saying and doing things that would provoke anger and – in situations where this was unavoidable – try to predict and prepare myself for her reactions. I also believe my inner critic was trying to protect my relationship with my mother, one of the most important relationships in most people's lives. I internalized the message: Your mother would be happier if you were different and tried to predict and pre-empt who my mother wanted me to be, rather than who I am.

I'm not alone in having a harsh inner critic that mirrors a parent. As psychologist Margalis Pjelstad writes in an article for *Psychology Today,*

> "I think our inner voice is started by whatever the parent say – whether it is loving, angry, encouraging, or critical."

As a child, we're deeply sensitive to the messages we receive from the people around us, especially our parents and other primary caregivers. Although our inner critics can be influenced by bullying or criticism from our peers and other authority figures too.

Compared to other mammals, human beings have an

extra-long period of dependence on our parents before we're capable of fending for ourselves. We relied on the people who cared for us during infancy and childhood for survival; they provided us with food, shelter and protection when we were not able to provide these things for ourselves; this also means we needed them to *want* to take care of us. One way of ensuring this was to please them, or at least to try to predict what would please them.

So adopting and internalizing the messages, rules for living and beliefs we got from our parents isn't just something that happens by coincidence – it's an effective survival mechanism. We are wired to do what we can to win their love and attention, including adopting their beliefs and internalizing the messages they mirror to us. As psychologist Sue Gerhardt writes in *Why Love Matters*:

> "Both our physiological systems and our mental systems are developed in relationship with other people – and this happens most intensely and leaves its biggest mark in infancy."

This is not a conscious process. Without even realizing, we attune to the key figures in our life and develop what psychotherapist Carl Rogers called "conditions of worth", a set of conditions we believe we must meet in order to be worthy of attention, care and love. When we internalize conditions of worth, we create rules for living which follow the formula: "When I do X, then I am loveable/worthy/acceptable". We internalize these rules so we can more easily follow them and therefore, in theory, more easily please those whom we depend on for survival. We also internalize self-beliefs based on how other people behaved toward, and treated, us during our formative years. These can range from conventional (if outdated) societal beliefs like "girls should be nice" or "boys don't cry", to more personally specific critiques. If you were frequently praised for being beautiful or criticized for being disorganized, you might have formed beliefs like "being organized means I'm more acceptable (and therefore being disorganized makes me unacceptable)" or "being beautiful makes me worthier (and therefore being average or unattractive makes me unworthy)". You might have also internalized messages about yourself and the world based on the beliefs your parents, extended family, authority figures or any of your other caregivers had about themselves.

> "When I'm overloaded with work, she says (she sounds like my mom): 'You should be working instead of . . .' but I try to negotiate with her because if I'm not alright, my work is going to suffer because of it."
>
> —Maryolin

Parents and other caregivers are most likely to become versions of your inner critics, but the genesis might also be someone else you've encountered on your journey through life so far. A writer I worked with realized her inner critic was a tutor from college who had vociferous beliefs about the right and wrong ways to be a "proper" writer. Even though she had only spent a short amount of time around this person and was already an adult when she reached college, this tutor – as an expert – was an authority figure and she had internalized his messages as truth. Years later, these beliefs still caused her internal conflict and criticism, as they were at odds with her own views on what she wanted to create and what being a proper writer meant to her. And this is one of the self-defeating aspects of the inner critic. Although it's trying to make us more – more successful, more likeable, more [*insert desired quality here*] – the way it goes about doing so erodes our self-confidence and influences our behaviour in a way that usually makes us *less* of these things.

As I explored the genesis of my inner critics, I realized that my inner critics were outliving their purpose. As an adult, I didn't rely on anyone else for survival, I didn't need to please the people whose voices I'd internalized anymore, nor did I need their acceptance or validation (although there was certainly a part of me that still craved it). Even so, my inner critics still talked as though I did. I was free. While other people's behaviour was, and is, their responsibility, my behaviour (including toward myself), my choices and the trajectory of my adult life was and is my responsibility, and mine alone.

Investigating the genesis of our inner critics isn't about finding someone (or multiple people) to blame. Blaming people who have wronged us in the past for our problems in the present gives them far more power than they deserve. Instead, it's about deepening your self-understanding so you can better take ownership and responsibility for improving your self-relationship and decide what you want that to look like going forward. So, rather than viewing my inner critic as this out-of-control voice that needed to be stifled, crushed, or numbed, I began to feel compassion for it. My inner critic had worked so hard to protect me from what it believed was a real physical and emotional threat: abandonment. And when I first understood how my critic had developed and grown to the gargantuan presence it had become in my life, when I looked inward and said, "Thank you for your hard work protecting me all these years," this is what I heard in response: blissful silence.

Our Inner Critics as Managers

When I was a teenager, I used to keep a page in my journal of hurtful things people had said to me as a reminder not to let my guard down when things were going well or I was feeling confident in my own skin. Although this was more self-defeating than anything else and my heart goes out to the girl who thought it was necessary to develop a thick skin, it was also an attempt to protect myself from future hurt. If I expected someone to say something mean or hurtful to me, it wouldn't be so surprising – and therefore devastating – when they did. It also reinforced an internalized message: *You deserve the bad things that people do and say to you.* Looking back from the perspective of adulthood, I would have encouraged my younger self to question why else people might have said those things: Were they having a bad day? Were the things they said a reflection of their own self-relationship? Did I misinterpret a comment that was actually neutral or even well-meaning? I also would have reminded myself to consider my feelings in the relationship too. As well as being concerned with what that person thought about me, to consider what I thought about them as someone who would say those things too.

While the ways I handle my inner critics are less self-punishing now, they still roll out the same old mantras whenever I try something new or something that takes me outside my comfort zone: beginning a new project, publishing a book, becoming a mother, moving to a new place and more. Over the last few years, I've had a few opportunities to do public speaking, something that simultaneously excites and terrifies me. I love the idea of public speaking and I love the feeling after I've done the speaking, but the bit in-between is hellish. Each time I have an upcoming presentation or workshop, one of my inner critics ramps up: *Who do you think you are to talk about this topic? You have nothing original to say. Everyone will be bored out of their minds and think you're a phoney. You will forget what you're saying halfway through, stumble over your words, and look like an idiot.* What's underneath it all is *I'm scared of rejection.*

This is another example of how my inner critic strives to protect me, by acting as what Internal Family Systems refers to as a "manager". Managers dislike intense emotions and so will do anything to avoid rejection, abandonment or other uncomfortable experiences. They are the parts that take over from our parents and other authority figures, keeping us in line and sticking to the script with which we were raised or – as I'll describe more in the section on primary and disowned selves below – railing against scripts we have unconsciously rejected.

As we explored at the end of the last chapter, when you peel back the layers of the inner critic, looking at when it becomes vocal and the things it becomes vocal about, you will often find that underneath its harsh words and destructive messages is fear. It tries to keep you small, to avoid potential rejection or criticism, and to avoid taking vulnerable or ego-threatening risks. In this way, your inner critics are trying to help you, albeit in their own misguided and counterproductive way. Although it can wreak psychological havoc and destruction, it's trying to protect you from its worst-case scenarios.

> "My inner critic's favourite story is that I am not good enough. Sometimes my inner critic will go so far as to tell me that I am a 'loser' and show me an imaginary perspective of myself as being feeble and disliked. My critic often tells me that I have mis-stepped and that others judge me for it and have decided that they don't like me. This has never been the case in reality."
>
> —Anita

Primary and Disowned Selves

Another way of envisioning how our inner critics fit with the rest of our internal dialogue is to think of it in the context of our primary selves and disowned selves. This is a concept developed by psychologists Hal and Sidra Stone, who describe primary selves as the "sub-personalities" or "identities" that make up what you think of as you. These are usually the aspects of our selves which were praised or valued by parents and other authority figures or role models. For example, you might identify with being responsible, romantic, high achieving, a perfectionist and so on.

As well as being influenced by the traits or identities that were valued when we were growing up, our primary selves can also develop as an inverse response to our parents' behaviour when we were growing up. One of my primary selves is calm and controlled – a doer who responds to crises and emergencies with an action plan and just gets on with it. I find it irritating when other people (as I perceive it) overreact to (what I perceive as) insignificant things. Growing up in a household where emotions ran unchecked and out of control, keeping a lid on my own feelings as much as possible became an anchor to cling to when things felt unstable around me.

Disowned selves are the parts of ourselves that are not allowed into our conscious lives. These are the identities or traits not tolerated or accepted by our caregivers (or those we don't tolerate in ourselves). They are the opposite of our primary selves and are also called our "shadow selves" (this is a concept we'll return to in Part II). As I mentioned above, one of my primary selves is calm and in control. Conversely, my one of my disowned selves is the version of me that expresses strong displays of emotion – negative and positive.

As you read about these two types of self, it might be hard to see the problem. So what if you have identities you prize and those you don't? Surely the primary selves are good things to have?

Well, not always. You might have developed primary selves that are actually unhealthy for you and detrimental to your personal and/or professional life (for example, my perfectionist primary self). When a certain primary self is in charge, that aspect of yourself is in control of your life; your decisions, your thoughts and our feelings, with little to no regard for the other aspects of yourself that make up the multitudes of who you really are.

And then there are the disowned selves. Even though

these selves are disowned, they still exist on an unconscious level. The problem with my calm and controlled primary self is that I end up holding in uncomfortable feelings until I can't anymore, at which point they erupt. Not only that, but as Brené Brown writes in her book, *The Gifts of Imperfection: Let Go of Who You're Supposed to Be and Embrace Who You Are,* we can't pick and choose which feelings we shut off. When we try to close ourselves off to so-called negative feelings, we close ourselves off to positive feelings too. This means I've also had to consciously allow myself to express the side of me that is spontaneous, fun-loving and playful more, something that can still feel vulnerable to do. Our disowned selves often manifest as the qualities, behaviours, or decisions we most often judge other people for– the judgement of others becoming a stand-in for judgement of ourselves. Remember how I mentioned that I find it irritating when I think other people are overreacting to seemingly insignificant things, and how I am prone to bottling up my own feelings until I explode over seemingly insignificant things? Case in point.

Disowned selves can be negative, but they can also include positive qualities. Those traits I mentioned above that might be primary selves for one person – responsible, romantic, high achieving, perfectionist – might all be disowned selves for another person (for example, someone who is capable but whose life is derailed by disorganization, self-sabotage, and poor decisions). These disowned selves still exist, and in certain contexts and situations they have a valuable role to play, but while they are unconscious, you cannot harness the power of these parts. Instead, they will pop out in an uncontrolled and untimely fashion, leaving you feeling mystified, out of control and even ashamed of your behaviour.

This is where the inner critic comes in. The inner critic strives to maintain equilibrium by promoting the importance of your primary selves and keep your disowned selves hidden away from the world. It pushes you toward the qualities of your primary selves and does its best to deter you from those of your disowned selves with little regard for balance, self-expression or your human complexity.

Drawing a Line Between Helpful and Hurtful

In the last two chapters, I shared how developing a deeper understanding of your inner critics, rather than ignoring them or calling them names, is crucial to developing a better relationship with this part of your internal dialogue. I also explained the difference between primary selves and disowned selves, and how the inner critic strives to maintain what it believes is the right equilibrium between the two. Although I found it useful to acknowledge how my it came into being and the purpose it served, I also reached a point in my exploration where I had to acknowledge that my inner critic – in its current form – was not good for me or helpful to my current life. As Hal and Sidra Stone explain in their book *Embracing the Inner Critic,* the inner critic *wants* us to have good things in our lives. It wants us to be happy, to have healthy relationships and to be successful – it just doesn't know when to stop – it snowballs out of control until it becomes destructive. It's also important to note your inner critic is *not* the same as your conscience or an inner compass of morality. Yes, its mission is to keep you in line with its rules for living, but these don't always correspond to your values or sense of right and wrong. The inner critic's aim isn't to help you transcend temptation and fallibility to make you a good person, it's to keep you safe by making you a small person.

When I let one or more of my critics take control, I behaved in ways that were self-sabotaging, even destructive. When I listened to and believed the voices that told me I was not good enough for this job or that relationship, I eventually (and unconsciously) proved those beliefs to be true through my decisions, words and actions. The more I believed my inner critics, the more I behaved in a way that represented who my inner critics said I was, the more ammunition I gave to their criticism and so reinforced the unhelpful beliefs.

Although it sounds simple, it's a truth that's easy forget: *Just because we think something doesn't mean it's true.* Some of my least proud moments and most painful memories come from believing what my inner critics were telling me and behaving in a way that reinforced those beliefs. This cycle is toxic and, to break it, you need to commit to stopping it here. It won't stop overnight – it might be something that requires your vigilance for the rest of your life – but changing the way you live, love, work and play starts with changing the way you talk to yourself. And that starts with being willing to do things differently.

Although it is trying to protect you (a mission that makes it so sticky and intractable in the face of argument, reason, the cold shoulder and hurling its abuse right back at it), your inner critics are working with beliefs that are no longer relevant to your current life and therefore no longer serve you. As we've explored, they might also be working with beliefs that aren't even yours to begin with, but those you've externalized from other people. The more aware you become of these beliefs, their sway over you and the impact they have on your life, the easier you will find it to say, "Thank you for sharing your opinion. I hear you are afraid of (*insert disaster scenario here*) based on the belief that (*insert belief here*). But this belief isn't relevant to my life now and I'm choosing to live based on the belief that (*insert new belief here*) instead." And you can say this with conviction, said in the knowledge these words are your truth.

Summary

In this chapter, we've explored where our inner critics come from. Developed early on in our lives, our inner critics play a special and, in some cases, necessary role. You might recognize a specific person or people within the voice of your inner critic and it's helpful to acknowledge this. The purpose of doing so isn't to blame or hold a grudge, but to be able to understand yourself better and begin to separate out your own values and beliefs from those your inner critic has internalized in the past so you can make conscious choices about who you are, what matters to you and how you want to live.

Before we move on to talking more about transforming your relationship with your inner critic, we're going to unpack some of the most common lies that your inner critic tells you. Knowledge is power and change starts with awareness, so the next chapter is about continuing to witness and befriend your inner critic.

Questions for Reflection

1. *What do you consider to be your primary selves? What traits or roles are important to you? How do you want other people to see you? What do you judge other people for, and how do you consider yourself to be the opposite of that?*
2. *What do you consider to be your disowned selves? What roles, qualities or traits do you judge in other people? Are there any people you value or admire around you whom make you feel inferior? What "selves" do these people embody that you don't embody yourself?*
3. *What are some of the things your critics most often criticizes? What consequences do they warn you about? List out as many as you can think of. If you aren't sure, try thinking back over the last 24 hours and recall some less-kind thoughts that came to mind about yourself. What were they?*
4. *Who (apart from your inner critics) has said these things (or similar things) to you? Who could you imagine saying these things?*
5. *What were your conditions of worth as you were growing up and into adulthood? These might be explicit expectations, for example around getting good grades or being well-behaved. It might also include unspoken expectations and roles, for example around being the family caretaker (or the family baby), or ideas you*

internalized from peers and authority figures about the "proper" way to be. List as many as you can think of.

6. *Return to the list in question 3 of things your inner critics have said to you. What do you think they might be trying to protect you from in these situations? If you look beneath their hurtful words and harsh criticism, how are they trying to help you?*

4

FIVE COMMON LIES YOUR INNER CRITIC TELLS

One of the most challenging and frustrating aspects of dealing with my inner critic is that sometimes I'm not even aware it's my critic that's talking. My critics are skilled at coming up with different ways of being heard and attempting to maintain control over my life. As well as sounding aggressive and belligerent, you might find your critic appears as a voice that seems rational and reasonable on the surface. If you unpack its dialogue and the underlying message, though, you'll soon find the same outdated beliefs, values and scripts lurking below the surface, along with the desire to keep you safe – whatever that looks like to your critic. The inner critic is adaptive, so if you've tried to ignore it or reject it, it might well have just changed tactics. When this happens, the voice in your head might not be shouting so loud anymore, but the deleterious effects of the inner critic I described in Chapter 2 will still show up in your life. So you can become more aware of the different ways in which your inner critic can try to control you, in this chapter I'm sharing five of the most common lies you might hear from your critic.

1. You'll Be Good Enough When . . .

The "you'll be good enough when . . . [*you lose 10lbs/get that promotion/can afford that car/get that degree/etc.*]" mantra is pernicious and can appear in several guises. One of these is "when . . . then . . ." thinking. For example, "When I get that dream job, then I'll feel successful/When I have the ideal partner, then I'll feel happy/When I buy that gorgeous dress I saw online, then I'll feel beautiful." The tricky thing about this thought pattern is that it doesn't always sound like a criticism. In fact, sometimes, it sounds more like "Yeah, go you! You get that job! You find that partner! You buy that dress!"

The problem with the meaning underlying all of the above, is that it tells you, "You are not good enough as you are." Well, hello there, inner critic. The fact is, you might feel successful if you get that job. But that doesn't mean you are by default *un*successful right now. You might feel happy if you find the right person to share your life with, but that doesn't mean you are destined to be *un*happy if you don't. You might very well feel gorgeous/confident in that new dress, but that doesn't mean you *won't* be gorgeous or confident without it.

And? The chances are – even if you get the job, find the partner, or wear the dress – you still won't feel successful, happy or beautiful. Because as soon as you have these things, the goal posts move. Now, it's not the job; it's the promotion. It's not the partner; it's having a house and a car and kids. It's not the dress; it's changing your hair, or losing a few pounds and so on.

Here's the truth: *You will never be good enough for your inner critic.*

This doesn't mean you will never be good enough, period. Good enough is subjective and part of transforming your relationship with your inner critic is taking back the reins and deciding for yourself what "good enough" means to you, rather than leaving it up to the frightened, out-of-control, unreasonable voice in your head. Remember your inner critic sets the bar high, unattainably high, because it's trying to keep pushing you into this state of perfection that makes you immune to judgement from other people (something it has an unrealistically negative lens about) – even though such a state doesn't exist in reality. You, on the other hand, are capable of a much more balanced, nuanced perspective of what "good enough" means. Not based on a feeling of scarcity or FOMO (fear of missing out), not based on other people's decisions and choices, not based on what you've been told you *should* do to be good enough, but based on your own values, your own moral compass and your own path.

I've found "good enough" is a shifting bar that changes depending on the day, what is happening in my life, my energy levels, my emotions and many more factors. It isn't set in stone; it's an agreement I make with myself and can use the support of my inner mentor to facilitate. We'll talk about this more in Part II.

2. Without Me, You'll Never Get Anywhere

As I've already mentioned, I have several critical voices in my head. There's the one who carries a thinly veiled fear of abandonment, telling me point blank that I can't do certain things because people will judge and reject me. There's a rage-filled shaming voice, who tells me all the things I should be ashamed of, that I deserve whatever is coming to me (except the good things – I don't deserve those!), and that I need to be someone other than who I am. If people knew what I was really like, they would run a mile.

Then there's a voice I call my inner taskmaster. My inner taskmaster tells me I need to work harder, faster, and better. While the inner shamer tells me I am not enough, the inner taskmaster whispers (or shouts) that I don't do enough, and maybe if I did more my inner critic would disappear and I'd finally feel good enough. (Notice how many of these inner-critic messages thread together?) It also comes up with countless variations on lie number two: you need me to push you; without me, you'd sit on your behind watching Netflix and eating Ben & Jerry's all day (it doesn't matter how many times I argue I don't even like that kind of ice cream, apparently that's not the point . . .), and so on. I took a good 20-plus years to recognize this strategy wasn't working. Given there are only 24 hours in a day and only so much coffee one person can drink, this wasn't a sustainable approach.

It's only in the last few years I've shifted away from believing I need to be hard on myself to get things done to a more positive, proactive approach. My previous motivational style was rooted in fear: *if I don't work as hard as I possibly can, how can I keep up? How can I believe I am enough?* My inner taskmaster met its match in my inner perfectionist. The kind that leads to workaholism paired with procrastination, fear of failure and underachieving. While these things are self-sabotaging, once again they are rooted in a desire for self-protection. I would leave projects and work until the absolute last minute, then reassure myself that, if the recipient didn't like what I'd done, it was because I had run out of time, not because I wasn't good enough. I would apply for jobs way below my skillset because I knew I could do them well, I wouldn't risk discovering I was no good and would be safer from criticism. I would try new things once then give up because I wasn't as good at them as people who had been doing them for a year or more (and, I rationalized, therefore never would be). In short, I had what is known as a "fixed mindset", a term first coined by psychologist Carol Dweck. Shifting from this fixed mindset to a growth mindset is part of the role of the inner mentor we'll be exploring in Part II.

As I engaged in more self-exploration, I learned more about the origins of my self-punitive approach to work and realized it was a reaction to values I'd internalized during childhood – values that weren't mine – rather than a reflection of what was healthy and the life I wanted to create for myself as an adult.

Much of changing my approach to work and fun has been around shifting from a fixed mindset to a growth mindset and from avoiding pain (in the sense of not being enough) to seeking growth (wanting to expand my skills, experience and grow as a person). Like most of the personal transitions I share in this book, this is still very much a work in progress. My inner taskmaster still tells me I need to be doing more and I have to be mindful of not letting it take the driving seat. Equally, I know my perfectionist still discourages me from doing things I want to do. I know it's my responsibility to go ahead and do them, anyway. In Part II of this book, you'll discover a different part of your internal dialogue – the inner mentor – that can help you with this.

It's also worth remembering this: of course your inner critic will tell you that you need it! After all, you're doing all these things, coming up with all these big ideas and daring to dream all these big dreams every single day that send it into a flurry of panic and fear. This isn't your fault; it's your place to do, think and dream big. But remember your inner critic thinks it needs to protect you. It wants to stick around to do its job and it truly believes that your life would crumble without it. It's also important to remember the mantra: *Just because your inner critic says it, doesn't mean it's true*. In fact, if your inner critic says it, it's almost certainly *not* true.

You do not need your inner critic – in its current form, anyway. As we'll discuss later, your inner critic has its uses and there are ways you can encourage it to turn down the heat and support you with a more tempered ways of expressing its fears and concerns.

3. Only You Struggle with This/Feel This Way

Ah, isolation. If your inner critic were a person walking around and speaking to you like it does in the real world, you would likely describe that person as abusive. And trying to make out you're the only one who is crazy/weird/stupid/ridiculous/whatever enough to feel this way or struggle with whatever your struggling with is one of the oldest tricks in the abuser book. As psychologist and researcher Brené Brown has explained in many interviews, shame thrives in secrecy. That's why abusive people often isolate their victims: to increase their potency. Like the "when . . . then . . ." thinking I described earlier in this chapter, this belief, that you are the only one going through what you're going through, is pernicious because it doesn't *sound* like your inner critic, but it is.

Here's the truth: there are over 7.5 billion people in this world and counting. Whatever you are going through, chances are you are not the only one.

Something that helped me question this story was remembering that even the most challenging and uncomfortable experiences I have are far more common than I might think. When I'm having a bad day, I make a mistake or my inner critic is running wild, it's tempting to look at other people with their successful lives, beaming smiles, and peppy social media updates, and think I am the only one in the whole wide world experiencing this right now. But that's my inner critic talking. In her book, *Self-Compassion,* Kristen Neff explains that the Latin root of the word compassion means "suffering with", and that these darker, more uncomfortable aspects of the human experience are threads that connect you and I to everyone else in the world. Even if the external situations around us differ wildly, our feelings, fears, hopes and dreams are things we share with others and the things that connect us all. If we're willing to bring them to light, they can bring us closer together too.

4. You Must Be Special/Fit In

Which one your inner critic goes for will depend on your culture and upbringing. If you live in a culture like the USA, it's the former. In other cultures (such as some European cultures), you're more likely to experience tall poppy syndrome (where people perceived as superior are more likely to be resented, criticized and cut down). Standing out is discouraged and criticized. Being ordinary is more than okay – some of your most special and meaningful life experiences will come out of "ordinary" moments and daily life. But if you have big things – goals and dreams – that's fine too. As long as they are motivated by what you want, not by needing to feel special, good enough, because of FOMO or because of any other negative-rooted, striving-based reason.

5. Everyone Will Think . . . /No One Will Like You

Life coach and author Martha Beck calls this kind of language "the generalized other". The generalized other shows up in sweeping statements such as, "Everyone will think this", "No one will like that". It's our social fears and anxieties projected onto the world and everyone in it. In my experience, I can unpack "everyone" and "no one" and trace them to one of two origins.

The first is that there might be specific individuals underneath "everyone" whose opinions or judgements I fear. And here's the rub: people *will* judge you, whatever you're doing in life. You could be the best in the whole wide world at what you're doing and there will still be someone, somewhere who doesn't like the way you're doing it (or the fact you're doing it at all). That doesn't make them right or wrong, it's just their opinion. Something I've had to learn and relearn is that if someone disagrees with me, or criticizes me, that doesn't mean they're automatically right. Sometimes they are, but more often than not, it's a difference of perspective, preference and values. They are free to have their ideas about the way I should do things and I'm free to have mine.

When I dig underneath the generalized other, the second origin I often find is my own judgements about myself. Other people's judgements don't matter half as much when I'm not judging myself for the same thing. Whenever I have the thought, *Everyone is going to judge me for...* or *Everyone will think* . . . I find it helpful to ask, "How am I judging myself for this? What does my inner critic have to say about it?" Other people's judgements are stickiest when they match how we judge ourselves. Remember the concept of the primary and disowned selves? As you now know, our inner critics are most pernicious when they're there, whispering critical nothings into your ear and we don't even realize it. Worrying about, or fearing the generalized other, is a sign you might be hearing your inner critic in disguise.

Whatever the origins of your generalized other, we often think people will notice far more than they actually do. It's a little-remembered fact that people are usually far too concerned with what's happening in their own lives to pay detailed attention to what we're doing in ours. I've also found it helpful to shift my perspective away from being blinkered on me and my feelings and consider other people's too. Is it fair to assume the worst of everybody?

How would I feel if I knew someone I cared about thought I was sure to judge them? One of my favourite mantras (and one I created for this reason) is "Assume the best". This helps me check any negative assumptions that pop up about the generalized other and gives me the space to choose how I want to approach other people: as adversaries to be feared, or as companions and collaborators on a shared journey?

Summary

In this chapter, you've unpacked some of the commonest mantras your inner critic might roll out, including its justifications for why you need it to exist. By becoming more aware of these, I hope you'll be able to recognize them when they pop up and separate fact from fiction. Remember, these statements are rooted in your inner critic's own fears and insecurities. They are not the truth and not a reflection of who you are. You are more than just your inner critic and so much more than the things it says about you.

In the next chapter, you'll learn more about why your inner critic is so attached to these lies, what's underneath them all and begin to heal your relationship with yourself.

Questions for Reflection

1. *What stories does your inner critic tell you about when you'll be good enough? What conditions does it set?*
2. *Write out a list of beliefs your inner critics currently act from. You can add to this list over the next days,*

weeks and months as you identify new beliefs. Then, work through each belief and ask yourself: What do I want to believe about this? What is the truth here? Replace each outdated or no-longer-relevant belief with an alternative set of beliefs you want to live by in the present.

3. *How have your inner critics influenced your behaviour? List two or three specific examples you can think of. How do you feel reflecting on those examples now? What would you do differently if you could go back and relive those situations?*

5

INNER CRITICS NEED HUGS TOO

My inner critics can be scary. When I think of the times I've tried to stamp out, shut down or drown out my inner critic, it's been because I felt overpowered and out of control. In response, I've tried to shut it down, to put the lid back on the box out of which it sprung. But this is part of the problem: it's trying to tell me something and I'm not listening. When I think of the times I've been in the same position – trying to reason someone I care about out of doing something I believe will very, very bad for them and getting nowhere – I can relate to how my critic feels: frustrated, misunderstood, invisible, mixed in with concerned, worried and just wanting them to be safe.

> "If you asked me to draw a picture of myself, I'd draw two. One . . . a happy, self-confident, regular-looking woman . . . the other . . . a giant gaping mouth that's ravenous for love."
>
> —Cheryl Strayed, *Dear Sugar*

If you want to experience greater understanding, tolerance and compassion in your life and the world around you, this starts within your relationship to yourself, including your inner critic. Having unpacked the complex workings and origins of your inner critics, in this chapter you'll explore how to create a more harmonious and constructive relationship with yourself – one founded on respect, understanding and self-compassion. You'll discover tools you can use with your inner critic to not only turn down the volume on the hurtful and unhelpful things it says, but also to strengthen other, kinder, parts of your internal dialogue, and so pave the way for deeper self-acceptance and self-compassion. This chapter sets the stage for Part II where you'll learn more about the inner mentor – an internal counterpart to the inner critic that provides supportive nurturing and mentorship based on your values.

In the previous two chapters, we looked at the origins and motivations of our inner critics and discovered why referring to them as "monsters" or "gremlins", while understandable, isn't fair. While your inner critics (in their current forms) are not helpful parts of your internal dialogue, they are working with what they believe to be your best interests in mind. Your critics see you teetering on the edge of a step and believe it's a cliff face. The critics shoulder a lot of responsibility for your wellbeing, but because they are born out of external criticism, unmet needs, and even abuse, they lack the emotional tools and templates to do so in a constructive and caring way. I already introduced the idea your critics have the emotional self-regulation of toddlers and the verbal acuity of adults. Like a toddler overwhelmed by feelings, screaming, shouting and expressing a whirlwind of emotion, the onslaught of an inner critic can also feel overwhelming and uncontrollable. While most parents dread toddler tantrums, a growing number of child educators and specialists believe tantrums are a sign a child has become overwhelmed by intense emotions they don't know how to handle and express appropriately. If a young child were acting out because they were overwhelmed by experiences they were struggling to process and deal with, how would you respond? With shushing, threatening punishment or ignoring them? Or by helping them process and express their feelings in a more constructive way?

The same principle applies to your inner critic. You have a choice: tell it to shut up, ignore it, call it names like "gremlin" or "monster", or recognize it as an immature, adaptive part of yourself that has valid feelings and opinions, which is trying to help (albeit in a counterproductive way), and needs firm but compassionate coaching to express itself more constructively. If you've tried the former approach, you'll find chastising your inner critics only makes them more vocal and belligerent.

The truth is you don't want to stamp out your inner critic altogether. Although it might feel hard to believe, your inner critics can be helpful in certain circumstances. You'll discover how and when in more detail in Chapter 9. For now, let's look at how you can begin to mend your relationship with your inner critics. Cultivating a more harmonious internal dialogue will make you better placed to use your inner critic to your advantage in the right situation.

> "A second characteristic of the process which for me is the good life involves an increasingly tendency to live fully in each moment."
>
> —Carl Rogers, *On Becoming a Person*

Beginning the Healing Process: Awareness

When I first became interested in personal growth, I had lived with a vocal inner critic for so long I wasn't even aware of it anymore. Part of my healing process involved deepening my awareness of my critics before I could go any further. I've already covered aspects of this awareness in previous chapters and will summarize them here:

- **Awareness of *when* your inner critics speak up:** What do they say? How do they communicate with you? You might find it helpful to refer to the list of inner critic behaviours in Chapters 2 and 3.

- **Awareness of *why* your inner critics speak up:** Which situations and experiences are most likely to provoke them? What are your most common inner-critic triggers?

- **Awareness of *where* the inner critics come from:** Who do your inner critics sound like? Which beliefs, values or stories from your past or present have you internalized? Which are yours and which belong to other people?

- **Awareness of *how* your inner critics influence your behaviour:** What do you change about your behaviour when you believe your inner critics? What do you do or not do because of what they say?

So how can you develop this awareness in your day-to-day life? It takes practice. Initially, this practice will be retrospective. You might be on the other end of an inner-critic attack when you realize what's happened. You might look back on the day gone by and recognize the times that your inner critic took charge. Starting with situations from the day or week gone by, trace your inner critic attack back to the source. When did your critic first speak up? What were you doing, saying or thinking about? What was the exact thought or memory that provoked your inner critic? Why do you think it took charge at that point? What was it protecting or defending in its own way?

As I've already mentioned, one of the most helpful tools I've used for this kind of reflection is journaling. The act of writing my responses to the questions above has helped me see my inner critics from a different perspective and gain some much-needed emotional distance from the things they say. Doing this has also allowed me to map out my answers to these questions with greater clarity than if I were to think through my responses. I've found journaling to be an excellent way of both deepening my self-awareness and keeping track of my personal growth – and the imperceptible progress that's hard to identify on a day-to-day basis but becomes clear over the longer-term. After a matter of days or weeks, it gives me a reference point to which I can look back and see how far I've come. I share more journaling exercises you can use with your inner critic in my book, *The Ultimate Guide to Journaling*.

Once you're able to gain awareness of the inner critic in retrospect, you can practise moving that awareness into the present. I've found this to be an ongoing process that ebbs and flows; some days I am more present than others, and on those days it's easier to notice when my inner critics are showing up unhelpfully. But overall, the more familiar I've become with how my inner critics work, the things they say and the situations that often provoke them, the easier it has become to be aware of them in the moment.

At the same time, my inner critics don't always say things that are obviously criticisms and this can make them hard to recognize. As I've already described, once your critics realize the jig is up, they'll find ways to maintain control under the radar. One way my inner critic shows up in disguise is through procrastination and resistance. When faced with a new project or idea, the conscious thought that comes up in this situation is, *I'm not ready, I need to wait.* When I dig deeper and ask why, out it comes: *If you try to do this now, you will fail. You'll be a joke. It's a total waste of time for you to even try. Who are you to do something like that?* Underneath, it's classic inner critic.

What separates inner-critic-related procrastination and resistance from garden-variety resistance is the energy behind it. Resistance comes in many flavours and from many sources, but inner-critic-related resistance has a sharp edge and undermining message to it: *You're not good enough, so you shouldn't even bother trying.* Identifying non-critical manifestations of the inner critic, which don't seem like criticism but come with the same undermining and "not good enough" energy, is an ongoing process. This is ninja-level critic-wrangling that takes time, patience and self-awareness. But being willing to explore our self-justifications for why we can't (or shouldn't) try the things we'd like to pursue – the ideas, callings, curiosities and dreams – awards us freedom that is well worth the effort.

Sidestep the Spiral of Self-recrimination

I'm walking down the street and my thoughts drift to a conversation I had with a friend the evening before, in which I said something that came out awkwardly and not as I had intended. As I think more about the situation, my thoughts start to descend into a doom-and-gloom disaster scenario: *She's going to think you were criticising her, she's bound to be offended . . . in fact, she's probably talking to her partner* ***right now*** *about how weird you are and how she doesn't want to be friends with you anymore!*

My inner critic is taking over, although I'm so lost in its stories I don't even realize. Then, another thought rings through, clear as a bell, *Oh, come on, this again? You know better than this, you're just not trying! Didn't you* ***just*** *read a book about this? What was all that therapy for if you're still getting stuck on things like this? You need to stop this self-indulgent BS. Grow up!* It's an inner-critic pile-on. Not only is my critic taking control of my thoughts about the evening before, but it's also admonishing me for the fact it *exists.* I briefly introduced the spiral or recrimination earlier in the book, and it's a common experience with our inner critics.

The spiral of self-recrimination looks like this: we self-attack, then self-attack for self-attacking, then self-attack for self-attacking our self-attack, then self-attack for self-attacking our self-attack our self-attack . . . and on and on into infinity. This is just another way the inner critic justifies its existence – to turn on itself. Because, if you experience an inner-critic attack, then obviously you need an inner critic to keep you in line and protect you from that in the future, right? That's inner-critic logic for you.

Like most aspects of transforming my relationship with my inner critic, I've found that noticing when I'm entering the spiral of self-recrimination is one of the most important steps because, once I recognize I'm there, I can extricate myself. First, I name it without judging myself or trying to fix it: "Oh, this is the self-recrimination spiral." It's not a life-changing statement, but it shifts my focus from "Argh, I should have this all figured out by now!" to naming what is and accepting where I'm at – rather than focusing on what I should or shouldn't be doing. More often than not, this relieves the pressure and helps me snap out of it. Being able to name the spiral without telling myself I shouldn't be in it, or judging myself for being so, transforms the energy of this interaction because I'm modelling self-acceptance. At this point, if my inner critic is still telling me about all the ways in which I'm failing at this whole personal growth thing, I can call on my inner mentor – a process we'll explore in more detail in Part II – to offer a more compassionate and fair perspective.

Gaining Emotional Distance

You have your own unique relationship with your inner critics. You might experience them as irritating voices that pop up every now and again but you can brush away with relative ease. Or, you might experience inner-critic attacks as paralysing and debilitating, leaving you mired in self-doubt and unsure how to move forward. Remember, this process isn't about eradicating or erasing your critics. Expecting yourself to do so can give your critics more fodder: *We're still here, so you're obviously not doing it right!* Instead, I encourage you to work *with* your inner critic, to notice the story it's telling you and say, "Thank you for your opinion, I'm listening *and* I'm still going to move forward with this." Like awareness, emotional distance is a way of thinking and relating to your inner critics that takes practice. These qualities of awareness and distance are important as they can help you realize that while your inner critics are part of you, they are just one of many different parts. They are not *you* and they don't define you or represent you as a whole.

Here are three tools I've found helpful for creating more space between myself and the things my inner critics say. None of these tools try to change what my critics are saying or convince myself to feel differently about them. Instead, they are about witnessing my thoughts and feelings and creating space for self-acceptance:

I Notice . . .

Reframing your critics' assertions with this (for example, "I notice I'm telling myself everyone is judging me negatively," or "I notice my inner critic is telling me I'm not good enough" can help you get some much-needed emotional distance from this internal voice. It's a short and simple phrase, but "I notice" can help you become an observer of your thoughts rather than a participant in them. This is especially the case if you tend to accept what your inner critics say as truth without question.

When I frame what my inner critics say with "I notice . . ." I can practise watching their statements float by without believing them but also without judging them or trying to shut them down. It allows my critics to express themselves, but within a safe container.

Ouch!

Saying to yourself "Ouch!" whenever you're aware of harsh self-talk is a way of acknowledging the impact your critics are having on you without getting caught up in trying to argue with them or prove them wrong. The act of stopping and saying this out loud (or muttering it under your breath) can help snap you out of a critic spiral and creates space for a more constructive and self-compassionate part of your internal dialogue to emerge (such as your inner mentor, whom you'll get to know better soon).

I first heard about using this phrase as a way of diffusing tension during arguments, but I've found it useful for taking the heat out of what my inner critic is saying and remembering to empathize with myself rather than buy into its stories.

In Your Opinion . . .

In the TV show *The Good Wife*, a recurring judge character insists the defence and prosecution frame their arguments with the phrase, "In my opinion . . ." rather than stating them as facts like they usually do. Any statement of fact is met with the following interruption:

"Is that your opinion?"

"Well, yes . . ."

"Then say. 'In my opinion.'"

While this is a comic character quirk, it's also a turn of

phrase you can started using with your inner critics (and outer critics – although perhaps just in your head). Framing my critics' statements with "In your opinion . . ." helps take the heat out of what they are saying and reminds me they are just one of many parts of my internal dialogue. And, like fictional attorneys on TV, just because they have an argument or an opinion doesn't mean it's a fact.

As well as gaining emotional distance, you will likely find being able to name and acknowledge your feelings and thoughts brings its own sense of relief. Doing this might not change the thought or feeling but recognizing what's happening can lessen its intensity.

Connecting with Healthy Anger

As I described in Chapter 3, an important part of healing my relationship with my inner critics has involved acknowledging and processing their origins. I've also talked about how it's our responsibility as an adult to do what we need to do to process and move forward from these experiences. Although it's important to identify the genesis of your inner critic – and be honest about your genuine experiences of the relationships that feed or are feeding it – doing so isn't about blaming the person or people whose voices you've internalized. You are allowed to feel angry for emotional experiences and support you needed and didn't receive as a child (or adult). You are also allowed to feel angry if you experienced punitive discipline, shaming, withdrawal of affection, verbal, physical, emotional or sexual abuse, or any other behaviours that are toxic within relationships. Even as an adult, it's difficult to take an objective look at an authority figure from your childhood and beyond, especially your parents, and see them as they truly are – flaws and all – and the impact their decisions and behaviour has had on you. Doing so can still feel threatening, like you're breaking an unspoken rule or being disloyal. But doing this, either on your own or in a safe space with the help of a counsellor, is a necessary part of healing your relationship with yourself. As psychotherapist Jasmin Lee Cori writes in *The Emotionally Absent Mother,*

> "(Anger) . . . is part of coming to your own experience, which sometimes differs from the family myth. Now as an adult, anger comes when you say, 'This was my experience, and what I got was not enough.'"

At the same time, whatever happened in the past, you and I are each responsible for our lives in the present. You are responsible for where your life is now. You are responsible for developing a better relationship with your inner critic. No one else can take over the job of accepting and understanding you in lieu of you doing that yourself. No one else will give you the acceptance and validation you are craving from yourself. Whatever you're looking for from people around you, ask yourself first: "Am I giving myself this?" You are the person who will make a difference.

This starts with taking charge of your environment. I've internalized specific voices because I've craved acceptance and approval from that person. While I was still hooked on wanting to get that acceptance and approval, it was impossible to turn down the volume on that inner critic or transform it into a more constructive, helpful part of my internal dialogue. Contrary to much advice about this topic, I don't think it's realistic or fair to expect yourself to stop looking for external validation altogether (I take it as a good sign if certain people who are positive influences in my life think well of me), but I do think it's important to be discerning about who you look to for approval. Not everyone is a good person to seek approval from – sometimes simply because they are looking at the world through a different lens than you. Part of transforming your relationship with yourself involves creating an internal validation filter, deciding individually, "Is this someone whose approval I really want?" Sometimes, it's not possible to do this on your own, in which case a good therapist can be a helpful ally. If your inner critic is an internalized version of someone who is still present in your life – and continues to be a vocal critic in your external world – it's important to set boundaries with them. I've included several useful books and articles on this topic in the Resources at the end of this book.

> "It's okay to be angry, even if what was done to you was unintentional. In fact, you have to be angry if you want to heal your wounded inner child."
>
> —John Bradshaw, *Homecoming: Reclaiming and Championing Your Inner Child*

Accepting Your Shadow Side

Although it's not always easy to admit, my critics often criticize me most for behaviours, thoughts, needs or wants I've disowned in myself. These are the traits and behaviours I was taught were not okay, for example communicating anger, expressing certain needs and being assertive with boundaries. They are also the traits I judge other people for: being irresponsible, being self-centred or self-indulgent, or rudeness. Learning to accept these shadow sides, the parts of myself I believe are unlovable or unacceptable, has been pivotal in taking away some of my critics' ammunition.

Unpacking your shadow side is like the process of identifying disowned selves. When exploring your shadow sides, one place to start is what annoys you in other people. Which traits and behaviours, when other people do them, leave you with an air of superiority and/or disdain? What bugs you, leaves you feeling outraged, or provokes an unwarranted degree of annoyance or frustration when you see other people doing it? Next, look at where you fear judgement from other people: how are you judging yourself for that?

Exploring your shadow side isn't just about looking at your less-desirable qualities, however. When I first became interested in personal growth, I went to a seminar hosted by a woman who was a self-proclaimed "life coach to the stars". Several women in the group were talking about comparing themselves to other people, and each time one of them talked about their experiences, the life coach would interrupt, saying, "You just need to stop it, you need to stop comparing yourself to other people." Someone would start sharing a personal story or situation and she would jump in, saying "Uh huh huh, that's you comparing yourself to other people. You need to stop that."

"So . . . *how* do we stop?" I asked.

"You just do. You just stop," she repeated for the umpteenth time, now sounding somewhat irritated. I left wondering if there was something I was missing. Comparison was plaguing my life at this time. I *wanted* to stop with all my heart and soul, so why couldn't I? Especially when this expert (and she is by no means alone in communicating this message) was saying it was that simple: I just needed to stop.

This question stayed with me for the next few years until I heard a coach called Tanya Geisler talk about the *golden shadow*. Up to this point, I'd been taking a "compare-and-despair" approach. I'd compare then despair, not only because I'd judge myself against other people and find myself lacking, but also because I thought I shouldn't be comparing myself to others in the first place; bad Hannah! (There's that spiral of self-recrimination again.) What Tanya explained was that comparison – like the inner critic – isn't something to be feared and avoided, nor is it something to stifle. Approached from a place of acceptance, comparison is a goldmine of insight and awareness about ourselves. We might put other people on a pedestal and feel we come up lacking in comparison. But if we dig down and specify where exactly we're comparing ourselves and what qualities we perceive ourselves as lacking compared to them, we have found our golden shadow: the feelings, traits or qualities that we want to embody more in our own lives. When we compare ourselves to other people, the particular aspects we focus on as part of that comparison are a signpost to unfulfilled potential in our own lives. We are capable of being these things too, it's just at some point we have disowned these traits within ourselves and adopted a different identity instead.

This perspective has transformed the way I approach comparison. Rather than being something I chastise myself for and try to push down, it's now something I approach with acceptance and curiosity. That's not to say I don't still compare and despair at times. I see a friend, a colleague or a public figure sharing photos of their life, describing a recent success or sharing a pithy wisdom bomb. And although I feel happy for them, there can still be a tinge of something bittersweet underneath that, a sense of inadequacy. Because my kitchen doesn't look that good, I definitely can't do handstand splits – let alone on a windy rock next to the ocean – I don't have a *New York Times* bestseller (yet), and I rarely feel as confident, sorted and creative as other people often seem to be. But when I dig down and specify where I'm comparing myself and what qualities I perceive myself as lacking compared to them, I've found my golden shadow. Those aspects I'm focusing on are a signpost to unfulfilled potential in my own life, unfulfilled needs and disowned selves.

Of course, comparison can also be based on outdated beliefs about how I *should* be living that I no longer agree with, and it's important to be able to tell the difference. For me, this appears as a difference in how the comparison feels physically. Potential-related comparison feels like sparks, a sense of longing, a desire for growth. Outdated comparison feels heavy, weighted and more like it's dragging me down than lifting me up. You'll find a list of questions you can use to explore the role comparison plays for you in Part II of this book.

Empathizing with All Parts of Yourself

I hope by now you understand the importance of practising empathy and understanding with your inner critic, treating them as you would wish to be treated yourself and accepting that – although unchecked they can do more harm than good – there is a method in the madness. They are acting in, what they believe to be, your best interests. There's another important reason to empathize with your inner critics, although it might seem counterintuitive. Finding empathy for your critics can also help you get emotional distance from what they're saying. When you recognize what you're hearing is the ramblings of a small, scared part of you that has learned to yell to get your attention, you're better able to look beyond its harsh words to the message underneath.

This doesn't mean ignoring your own feelings, though, and you need to be able to empathize with how you feel about your inner critics' words too. As I described in Chapter 1, a dominant inner critic causes internal polarization. This is when two parts of your inner dialogue conflict with each other. Even though you are no longer a child, your inner critic triggers another part of yourself that is childlike in its emotional responses and reactions to the inner critic. If you think about how you feel when your inner critic attacks you, it might be helpless, defenceless, overwhelmed, scared, ashamed and disempowered. It becomes consumed by shame and blame, which results in the self-sabotaging, even self-destructive behaviours I mentioned in Chapter 2. So, to develop a more harmonious internal dialogue, you need to empathize with both your inner critics *and* your inner child. It's important to gain a deeper understanding of what your inner critics are trying to tell you, but this doesn't mean accepting everything they say or letting them rampage unchecked. Like any relationship, boundaries are important. I wouldn't accept a friend or partner telling me I'm lazy, no good and worthless, and I'm not helping myself by accepting that from my inner critics either.

At the same time, I also need to be able to tolerate any strong feelings I have in response to my critics, which are rarely comfortable. Just as my inner critics can feel overwhelming, so can the childlike part they trigger – which can leave me feeling helpless and victimized. Earlier, I described how I've found it useful to get emotional distance from my inner critics, and the same principle applies to my inner child. I've also needed to be able to create a mindful distance from the part of me that is reactive to my inner critics so I can tolerate its feelings without being overwhelmed by them. The same techniques I described earlier in this chapter have been useful for gaining distance from my inner critics have been invaluable for this too.

Although it might not feel like it right now, you have the power to set boundaries with your inner critic. This might begin as simply as gaining awareness using the statements above, like "The story I'm telling myself is . . ." or "I notice . . ." You might take a deep breath to calm yourself first, then say to your inner critics, "I hear you have something to tell me and I'd like to know what that is, but you cannot call me names or shame me like this. I want to hear your message and know what's happening for you but I can't when you're attacking me instead of telling me what's really going on. Can you please tell me what's happening for you without any of the extra language?" This is just an example for what works for me but you can tailor it to sound more natural to you).

When I first heard about this technique, I was sceptical; is it really as simple as asking? Often, yes. The best way to get my inner critics to calm down and work with me instead of against me is modelling what respectful and boundaried dialogue looks like. This didn't happen for me immediately, but with practice I noticed a shift in how I felt about my critics, how I responded to them and how they responded to me. Just because my inner critic was panicking didn't mean I had to panic too. Just because my inner critic was feeling fearful and overwhelmed didn't mean I had to join it there. The more I practised acceptance, boundaried kindness and curiosity, the more I began to trust my ability to respond to an inner-critic attack appropriately, and I found my critics started calming down and becoming less belligerent as a result.

Empathizing with all parts of yourself also means accepting you won't solve this the first time, or the thirtieth. As I've mentioned already, maintaining a constructive relationship with your inner critics might be something that requires vigilance and attention for the rest of your life. Part of changing this relationship involves avoiding expectations based on impossible standards, such as never feeling overwhelmed by your inner critic again, then criticizing yourself for feeling that way the next time your inner critic pipes up.

Your attempts to be kinder to yourself won't work every time. Sometimes it will take three or four tries. You might not feel any different in the moment – but when it comes to your inner critic, you need to be in it for the long haul. Like the other practices and exercises in this book, the aim isn't to *fix* anything about yourself but to create a new, kinder way of relating to all parts of your internal dialogue and yourself as a whole.

> "I recently have been struggling with the decision to pursue my pilot's licence. I hesitated for weeks on making the decision to go for it because the voice in my head told me I wasn't good enough, I could never succeed, and it would be too challenging. When I finally realized the only thing stopping me from succeeding was this voice, I decided to start telling myself I CAN do this. I AM good enough. It's an ongoing practice, but I'm no longer letting that voice make decisions for me."
>
> —Mallory

Becoming Your Own Leader

The TV show *The Dog Whisperer* with Cesar Milan is ostensibly a show about dog training, but watching a few episodes reveals it's as much about human psychology as it is about man's best friend (bear with me, because it's also relevant to our inner critics). Almost every episode involves the same issue: troubled dogs, exacerbated or created by troubled owners. More specifically, it involves owners not taking the leadership role and giving the dog what it needs while setting appropriate boundaries. Some owners treat their dog like they would a baby or a best friend, giving it cuddles, the run of the house and letting it do whatever it wants. Others take the polar opposite approach and are punitive. Others still are overwhelmed and have no idea how to handle the big, furry bundle of energy in front of them. In almost every episode, Caesar Milan explains how dogs don't need friends or companions, they need a pack leader. Without a pack leader, they go crazy – they bite, misbehave, bark at anyone and everything, and show all those dog behaviours that drive people up the wall – because they feel vulnerable. They sense the instability and lack of leadership in their pack. Without a calm but firm pack leader, they try to jostle for the position themselves to keep the pack safe. Part of responsible dog ownership is to be the pack leader.

Although it might seem like a strange comparison, your inner critics need the same kind of leadership. If you don't provide that leadership through cultivating a strong inner mentor – as we'll explore in Part II – your inner critic will try to step up and take on that role. Your critic needs a strong, positive, nurturing counterpart to take the lead, offer security, provide mediation and help you thrive. And that's what we're about to explore.

Summary

In this chapter, I've shared how to start dealing with your inner critics with greater respect and self-kindness, modelling the behaviour you'd like to see from them and encouraging them to rise to meet you, rather than sinking to their level. I've mentioned the different practices you can use to develop a healthier relationship with your inner critics, including awareness, gaining emotional distance, and phrases or mantras you can use to respond to them. I've also talked about empathizing with, while having boundaries with, all parts of yourself: your inner critics and polarized wounded child parts.

So where to from here? In the next chapter, you'll learn more about the inner mentor. Besides the practices I mentioned in this chapter, this is the internal voice that has had the biggest positive effect on my relationship with myself and helped me transform my relationship with my inner critic. Given the chance to be heard through the noise, your inner mentor can help you turn down the volume on your inner critic's not-so-helpful chatter, while still honouring and respecting the ways they can be an asset to your life. Are you ready?

Questions for Reflection

1. *Keep a diary for at least the next week or month, answering the questions below at the end of each day for the 24 hours prior:*

- *What behaviours or qualities do you judge in other people? How do you feel about these behaviours or qualities within yourself?*
- *What do you hope people never learn, realize or see about you? What do you not want people to know about you?*
- *Who do you most often compare yourself to? What qualities does that person have that you would like more of yourself? What potential is this comparison pointing to that you're not owning in yourself?*

II

INTRODUCING YOUR INNER MENTOR

"The thing that is really hard, and really amazing, is giving up on being perfect and beginning the work of becoming yourself."

—Anna Quindlen

6

WHAT IS THE INNER MENTOR?

As I became more conscious of my inner critic – when it showed up, what it said, and why it did what it did, I started to become more aware of the other voices that made up my internal dialogue too. One of these in particular was becoming stronger and more present the more I consciously worked on my relationship with my inner critic. This is the part I call my "inner mentor". This voice was like a wise, guiding figure: it had the same calm, confident presence I associate with the wisdom of insight and experience, it rarely told me outright what to do, but rather asked questions that helped me sort through my different options. I quickly realized I could trust this voice – it had my best interests at heart but, unlike the inner critic, could also communicate this in a compassionate and fair way. What I noticed most about my inner mentor was the energy it brought. When my mentor was present, I felt calmer and more grounded. Whatever was going on in the outside world, I felt confident in my ability to handle it.

In Part I, you learned more about of the biggest obstacles to self-compassion, internal peace and a life fully lived: the inner critic. In this section, you'll discover how the inner mentor can help you mediate with your inner critics and offer a more constructive and helpful way of approaching life's challenges and difficulties. I'll start by explaining the purpose of your inner mentor, how it can help you with your inner critics, and I'll share practices you can use to connect with and build a visual image of what your inner mentor looks like to you.

The inner mentor is described by Jay Earley and Bonnie Weiss within the Internal Family Systems framework as a part of our internal dialogue that is extrapolated from our inner critic, a healthier version of the critic itself. In this section, I refer to it as a separate voice as that's how I experience it. I've also found thinking of my inner mentor as separate from my inner critics useful for creating emotional distance and unhooking from the critics' control.

The description of the inner mentor that resonates most with me is similar to that portrayed by coach and author Tara Mohr in her book *Playing Big*. She presents the inner mentor as an antidote to feelings of self-doubt in relation to work and business, however the same principle applies to the rest of our lives too. When I first read this term in her book, it felt right; I finally had a proper name for this part of my internal dialogue. I've also seen and heard this part referred to as our "inner cheerleader", our "inner good girl" (as opposed to "inner mean girl") and more. However, I prefer the term inner mentor for two reasons. I believe this aspect of our internal dialogue is relevant to and vital for everyone, whatever their gender, and there are certain connotations and conditioning associated with the term "good girl" that don't align with self-acceptance and authenticity. Second, sometimes kindness (and self-kindness) means doing things that feel uncomfortable: taking ownership when I've wronged someone or behaved badly, making hard decisions and setting difficult boundaries. In these situations, thinking of this nurturing and supportive part of myself as the namesake of a pom-pom wielding athlete in a short skirt doesn't feel appropriate. Sometimes I do or say things that don't warrant cheerleading, but rather accountability, responsibility and making amends.

When I think of the phrase "inner mentor", however, I visualize someone who has wisdom, expertise and experience to share with me, and is invested in my growth and future, whatever that looks like. I imagine her as gentle but firm (rather than shouty and rah-rah) and with a deep well of resourcefulness, strength and resilience. Your inner mentor might look very different to you; perhaps you might not even wish to think of this part as your inner mentor at all but have a different name or label in mind. Later in this chapter, I'll share practices you can use to build a visual image of your inner mentor and connect with this part of yourself, but for now I want to emphasize there is no *right* way for your inner mentor to appear – create something that is personal and feels right to you.

The Purpose of Your Inner Mentor

The inner mentor is the antidote to the inner critic, and so much more. While the inner critic's aim is to avoid risk and vulnerability, keep you small and bully you into sticking to its rules for life, the inner mentor is invested in your growth and expansion, your wellbeing, and in you achieving your full potential in (and therefore fullest experience of) life. The inner critic tries to protect you at all costs, while the inner mentor encourages you to take reasonable risks in service of exploring your potential.

One way of thinking about this part of us is that it is like your ideal vision of a parent: nurturing, supportive, trusting, accepting, respectful, with belief in your capabilities and strengths. Consciously cultivating an internal part with these qualities could be especially helpful and healing if you didn't receive some of these qualities in childhood. Your inner mentor might also embody particular qualities important to you. Among other traits, my inner mentor embodies fairness, patience, integrity and courage.

Your inner mentor is there to help soften your self-judgements and self-criticism; it can provide objectivity, compassion, big-picture thinking, and much of what is missing from the inner critics.

Your Inner Mentor as Challenger and Coach

In Chapter 1, I described the Internal Family Systems concept of polarization, and how different parts of our internal dialogue can be triggered by, and be in conflict with, each other. An example of this is the inner critic provoking the childlike part of us that feels helpless, victimized, disempowered and overwhelmed. While the inner mentor isn't polarized with the inner critic, it is a counterpart and can firmly but compassionately challenge it. As I already explained, your inner mentor doesn't do this by telling your critic to get lost or to shut up, but by responding with boundaries, open-minded curiosity and rationality, all anchored in reality.

To return to an example I used earlier in the book, let's say you're preparing for a job interview and your inner critic starts telling you how much better qualified the other candidates will be, how awful you are at interviews, how ridiculous you'll look and asking unhelpful questions like, *Who do you think you are applying for this job, anyway?* Your inner mentor can remind the inner critic that this kind of chatter isn't helpful at this time. It can also ask what the inner critic is afraid of and what its worst-case scenario is –*That the interviewers will judge you? That you'll get the job and end up feeling out of your depth?* Your inner mentor can also ask what doing a good job at the interview would look like, how you can best prepare, and remind you of all the reasons you are a good fit for this job: all the skills and experience you do bring; the fact you're a hard worker, constantly looking to learn and better yourself (or whatever statements feel true for you). In this way, the inner mentor acts as an internal coach. Sometimes, the best coaching is based purely in enquiry and understanding, and I'll be sharing more inner-mentor questions you can adopt in the next chapter.

At the same time, the inner mentor's job isn't to be "nice". As a culture, we often conflate kindness with being nice, but they are two very different things. As coach Randi Buckley explained in an interview for the "Courage and Spice" podcast,

> "Nice is about comfort . . . Kindness transcends that and

> goes deeper into what really matters. It goes into the depth of caring about people, the world and yourself."

One of the definitions of nice is "pleasing"; in other words, how other people perceive you and whether they like you. Kindness, on the other hand, is "marked by ethical characteristics". True kindness embodies the words, conversations, behaviours and actions that prompt you to be the best version of yourself. It encourages you (*en-courages*, gives you courage) to live in alignment with your values and principles, even when doing so feels difficult. True kindness doesn't always feel comfortable in the moment; it might come in the form of a rejection, a much-needed pep talk, a long-overdue wake-up call. But true kindness always promotes truth and integrity over comfort. It's a pathway to a life lived fully lived, with deeper degrees of truth and authenticity. True kindness often diverges from what other people might perceive as "nice".

In the same way, I might not always like what my inner mentor has to say, but she speaks from a place of compassion, care and trust in my ability to do the right thing and be the best version of myself I can be.

Connecting with Your Inner Mentor

You can probably connect with your inner critic with little prompting; in fact, it can feel like it's just waiting for an opportunity to share its many opinions about what you're doing wrong and how you're screwing up. But what about connecting with your inner mentor? I have found two methods useful for bringing this part of my internal dialogue forward:

Think of Times When Your Inner Mentor Was Present

While it might not be as easy to think back to examples of your inner mentor's dialogue, a helpful way to connect with times this part has been present is to think back to times you felt a certain way. When have you felt grounded and like you were living in alignment with your most important values? When did you hear an internal voice comforting you, encouraging your nudging you forward with compassion, integrity and belief in your capabilities? When have you heard this voice encouraging you to do the right thing, even when it felt difficult or uncomfortable? What did this voice say? How did it sound? And how did you feel?

Visualize Your Inner Mentor's Appearance

I've found it easiest to connect with my inner mentor when I imagine her as a person. My inner mentor is an older woman, usually sitting in a chair, plump and cuddly with short, sandy hair and a soft voice. I can't see the exact features of her face but these aspects are enough for me to connect with this part of my internal dialogue. Perhaps your inner mentor is an older version of yourself: the person you would like to be at that age. This kind of visualization isn't everyone's cup of tea, so feel free to adapt it to something that feels more natural to you. Perhaps you see your inner mentor's presence as a colour or a physical feeling. You might also find it helpful to call up certain archetypes associated with wisdom and support, such as a wise sage, a crone or a guide. I'll explain the visualization process in more detail in the next chapter.

When Your Inner Mentor Is Nowhere to Be Felt (Yet)

Some people can connect to their inner mentors with relative ease. Reading this chapter, you might already identify times in your life when your inner mentor has stepped forward and taken control, steering you in a supportive and constructive way. If you're like me, however, it might require a little more creativity and work. Perhaps you're not sure what it looks like to be held accountable compassionately, gently challenged, and encouraged to show up, be visible and take up space in the world without being pushed.

Wherever you're starting from, know it is possible to cultivate a compassionate, nurturing inner voice. It won't necessarily be easy, it will take time, but you can do it. This isn't just motivational talk, it's backed up by science. As psychologist Rick Hanson describes in *Buddha's Brain*, our brains are made up of trillions of neural pathways; connections that form during childhood and adolescence. These pathways are well-worn patterns of thinking and behaviour we've developed during this time that we continue to use into adulthood. Your current way of responding to your inner critics – and even the critics themselves – are neural pathways. They are ways of habitual thinking you've been using for years. The more you use a set of pathways, the stronger and more deeply entrenched they become. Your brain is highly efficient, which means you will always default to the strongest neural pathway (the one with least resistance). This is why it takes effort and awareness to break unwanted habits.

The same goes for your thought patterns and your inner critics. The longer you allow your inner critics to roam unchallenged, the more deeply entrenched they become. But you can change these pathways.

Think of a neural pathway like a woodland path. If you take the same path through the woods every day that path will become well-worn and clearly visible. The more you use it, the smoother it becomes, and therefore the easier it becomes to walk along too. But let's say one day you arrive at the wood and decide you want to take a different path. You start where the first path starts but veer in a new direction through a different part of the wood. The first trip is tough going because you don't have a clear visual of where you're going – beyond where you're stepping next. You have to hack away at the plants and bushes in front of you and keep having to stop to remove the big rocks and boulders in your way. It's exhausting work and, because it's your first time on the new path, it feels strange. The next day, you return and face a choice: persevere with the new path or return to the relative comfort of the old one. You find yourself thinking how the old path feels much easier at this point. This is where what you decide to do next matters.

If you continue to persevere with the new path, it becomes easier and easier. With lack of use, the old path becomes overgrown and eventually disappears. Soon, it's as if it were never there in the first place and the newer, better path is the only way through the woods. If you return to the comfort of the old path, however, that path will continue to be the easiest, and each time you try to re-join the newer path, it will require a lot of effort to clear.

The same principle applies to your neural pathways. You can change them – you can change your response to a thought, you can sometimes even work to change the thought itself – but you need to be willing to make the effort and persevere. The first few times you do this, it will feel unnatural, uncomfortable, even scary. But the more you can sit with those feelings – without reacting to them and retreating to the comfort of the old pathways – the more natural and easier it will become. In simple terms, you're shifting from using the pathways dominated by the inner critic to the pathways that are the domain of the inner mentor.

Creating an inner mentor with the qualities I've discussed in this chapter so far can be challenging when you don't have a good template for what this looks like. In this case, it's helpful to have a framework with which to begin. This could come from something you've read, heard or experienced. Because my inner mentor is female, I like the 10 "good mother" messages Jasmin Lee Cori offers in her book, *The Emotionally Absent Mother*. As soon as I read them, I knew I wanted to adopt and internalize these messages and started to practise using them with my inner mentor.

Your own inner mentor messages might come from positive feedback you've received in the past, messages you've heard or read that particularly resonate with your, or other people's ideas and words or wisdom.

Summary

You will find more tools and suggestions to help you cultivate your inner mentor, wherever you're starting from, coming up next. In this chapter, I've introduced the concept of the inner mentor – what it is and how it can support you as you make your way through life. As well as being an antidote to the inner critics, your inner mentor's purpose is to ensure you stick to the values that matter most to you and to encourage you to be the best version of yourself you can be at any given time. Your inner mentor is rooted in self-kindness. Remember, this isn't the same as cheerleading, nor is your inner-mentor's role always to be "nice". Instead, he or she (or it) embodies the qualities that encourage you to be the best version of yourself – not motivated by fear of not being enough but from a place of wanting the best for yourself and wanting to explore what you're capable of being, doing and creating in the world.

In the next chapter, I'll share more about how to tell the difference between your inner critics and inner mentor, and how to cultivate self-acceptance while also honouring your desire for growth. Then, we'll talk more about the different ways you can turn up the volume on your inner mentor, strengthening this part of your internal dialogue and, in turn, your self-kindness.

Questions for Reflection

1. *What name resonates for you as you think about this aspect of yourself? What qualities would you like this*

part of yourself to have? What do you see his or her main role as? Finally, how do you imagine yourself feeling in the presence of your inner mentor? (For example, calm, held, supported, encouraged, challenged, seen, heard or whatever feels important to you.)

2. *Look at the list of feelings you wrote in response to the last set of reflective questions. When have you felt that way, especially within yourself? What was happening at that time? Who were you with? How were you talking to yourself? What prompted that self-talk?*
3. *What messages would you like your inner mentor to reflect to you? Which of those messages feel most important? What would you most like to hear from her or him?*

7

INNER CRITIC OR INNER MENTOR?

As I worked on my relationship with my inner critic and started exploring the importance of my inner mentor in improving my internal communication, I encountered a number of questions and seeming contradictions that took me some time to unravel and figure out. These were questions like:

- What's the difference between a healthy desire for growth and an unhealthy one?
- If there are things I want to change about myself, how does this fit in with self-acceptance?
- Surely if I accept myself as I am, then I don't want to change? So does that mean change is bad? I'm confused . . .

More than anything, I wondered how to reconcile a desire for growth with self-acceptance and compassion. How could I make sure I was approaching creating growth and change in my life from a healthy perspective? If my inner critic were to hijack a growth-related activity or project and take over, how could I tell the difference between inner-critic-driven growth and inner-mentor-driven growth? That's what this chapter is about.

Personal growth is full of paradoxes, and this one is up there with the best. If you're anything like me, you probably always have a running list of things you'd like to do, learn, change or shift about yourself or your life. When I first started learning about self-acceptance, I thought this desire for change was a sign I wasn't doing this whole self-acceptance thing properly (cue the spiral of self-recrimination I mentioned in Chapter 5).

Since then, I've realized that this desire for change is really a desire for *growth,* and this desire for growth is a very human desire we all share on one level or another. Many factors influence whether you experience growth and make the changes you want to make, but the underlying desire is there. So how does that fit with other important concepts like self-acceptance? Here is what I've learned about this dichotomy: *A healthy desire for growth is rooted in self-acceptance.*

It starts with acknowledging the reality of where you are now: whether that's in a relationship or career that's not working for you, dealing with a chronic health problem, in debt and so on. An unhealthy desire for growth starts here too, but what differentiates the two is how you respond to this reality.

Rooted in self-acceptance, we notice where we are; we acknowledge the situation; we acknowledge any feelings that come up about it (including shame, a wish that things were different and so on). If judgements come up, we acknowledge those too. This acknowledgement gives us emotional distance so we can take a step back and observe our current situation from the 30,000ft view. From here, we can see how we arrived at this place, where our responsibility lies and what needs to happen for us to move forward. And when we do move forward, it's motivated by the desire for a better future in whatever area of life we're addressing and by wanting the best for ourselves.

When we approach these kinds of situations with an unhealthy desire for growth, we do so from the place of "not good enough". We're motivated by pain and shame, by a fear of other people finding out just how not good enough we really are, and we listen to the voice in our heads that says, You *will be lonely forever, you're a loser*, etc. *ad nauseam*. In other words, our desire for growth is driven by shame.

The problem with shame is that it makes us more likely to want to hide and avoid, to cover up. Shame is anti-growth. Because we don't accept this flaw or situation, we assume other people won't accept it either. So we try to hide it and pretend it doesn't exist, it's not really a problem, rather than take steps to remedy a problem or create the growth we want. It's the difference between a crash diet before a school reunion and deciding to go to the gym three times a week to work on our fitness. Both actions might have the same result (-ish; the crash diet is unlikely to have any lasting effect on our weight and is unhealthier in the short term), but the energy and emotion behind them is very different. One is about avoiding pain (*people will judge me if they see me for the first time in years and I'm carrying around this extra weight*) and the other is about pursuing growth.

I used to do this with money. In my early twenties, I was in debt (not a lot by adult standards, but it felt like a horrendous amount to me). I was also part-time self-employed, part-time working in the charity sector (which isn't known for its amazing rate of pay). I was kind of, sort of, very slowly paying off my debt, but I was also making unhelpful financial decisions that were impeding my progress. Looking back now, I can see how these were motivated by shame: I felt ashamed of having debt. I felt ashamed of the choices that had led there (poor financial decisions, repeatedly lending money I didn't have to an ex-boyfriend and starting my self-employment without a savings buffer). So I tried to hide it, I tried to act as though it didn't exist, or at least as though I didn't feel as bad about it as I actually felt. Which meant rather than channelling all my energy (and spare cash) into paying off the debt, I behaved as though I didn't have any and everything was fine. Which left me with less money to pay off the debt.

This is the vicious shame cycle. As you might remember from Part II, your inner critic likely tells you that you need it, rely on it, to keep you in check. Mine certainly told me I'd never pay off my debt without it reminding me how shameful it was to be in the red on a daily basis – and this almost makes sense. Internal accountability is important and we all need some kind of moral compass. But the shame provoked by the inner critic is counterproductive to real, lasting change.

Our inner mentors provide us with this internal accountability in spades when we open ourselves to it, when we let it. First, this requires that we work on revealing and dissolving shame about ourselves, our lives and our past experiences. I needed to unpack my relationship with money (a process that continues today) and look at what wasn't working and why. I also had to shine a light on the darker areas of shame. Remember Brené Brown's message: "Shame thrives in secrecy"? This is never truer than in our relationship with ourselves. Shame can be difficult to work on alone, so if you're in a similar position, you might find it useful to enlist the support of a good counsellor or therapist who is well-versed in the havoc shame can wreak on our internal and external lives.

As we become more aware of and uncover where shame has its grip (and therefore the inner critic reigns), we can start to shift the driving force behind this desire for change. For me, this looked like uncovering the belief behind the shame (like most of my shame-based beliefs, this came back to some variation of "not good enough") and figuring out whether that belief was mine or based on someone else's values. When I started thinking about this in relation to money, I realized a lot of my shame was rooted in beliefs I had picked up years before – such as "affluence equals status, therefore appearing affluent is more important than being affluent" – rather than beliefs I agreed with myself. Recognizing these beliefs enabled me to unpack and explore my own values around money. What do I believe the purpose of money to be? What kind of a relationship with money do I want to have? It also enabled me to gain valuable insights into how money works in the real world and the dangers of common phenomenon such as lifestyle creep. But while I let my inner critic dominate my internal conversation about money with statements like, *You should have all this sorted out by now* (underlying message: and the fact you don't means you are a failure as a person), I wasn't open to exploring and learning about all of this.

Another way to gauge the difference in energy between the inner critic and the inner mentor is to notice how the change feels on a physical level. Try this as an experiment: think of something you hate doing. Perhaps this is something you need to do but you've been putting off for a while because it sucks; it's the worst, and you would rather spend the next two years filing your taxes than do this thing. When you think of that thing, how does your body feel? If you're anything like me, I feel a shard of tension in my chest, my shoulders become tighter and I feel a nervous kind of energy building in my core. Now think of something you love to do, something you look forward to as soon as you decide to do it, something that leaves you feeling happy, energized and optimistic about life. How does your body feel now? I feel feather-light in comparison. My shoulders relax, the tightness in my chest relaxes and I feel more energized. Your physical responses might be different in each situation, but the point is to notice the different physical energies that arise in each scenario. This is what people refer to when they talk about your "gut instinct". It's your body responding to years of knowledge, experiences, lessons and beliefs (some of which you might not consciously know of), with certain physical feelings. Our gut instinct isn't always right, but it's always worth paying attention to as it contains useful information – if not about the current situation, then about ourselves.

We feel the same kinds of differences when we experience thoughts and the desire for change fuelled by our inner critic compared to those fuelled by our inner mentor. The more you become aware of these physical responses – and the meaning behind them – the more you'll be able to notice the difference between changes that are driven by your inner critic and those driven by your inner mentor.

When we approach changes we want to make in our lives grounded in healthy values (and by healthy, I mean things like "integrity", rather than "wanting everyone to like me",) this is the domain of our inner mentor. And although the desire for change might look the same at the surface level, the energy behind change fuelled by the inner mentor is completely different compared to the desire for change driven by the inner critic.

This key difference is summarized by the difference between being driven by wanting to avoid pain and being driven by wanting to pursue growth. Like the inner critic, this difference isn't always easy to tell. For example, I sometimes fall into the trap of believing if I change this one thing about my life, everything will be different. I'll feel happier, the rest of my problems will dissolve like candyfloss in a stream, and I'll never have a bad day again! (This is an exaggeration, but that's the manic energy behind it.) While this might look like "pursuing growth", it's really the avoiding pain kind. If I believe "when I do X, everything will be different", X has become a scapegoat for everything I'm unhappy about in my life and a way for me to kid myself that making one change will save me from the pain of discomfort, vulnerability, rejection, uncertainty, and/or whatever else I'm trying to avoid, for the rest of my life. In reality, no external change can save us from ourselves. As the title of the bestselling mindfulness book by Jon Kabat-Zinn explains, *Wherever You Go There You Are.*

When our inner mentor is in the driving seat, change comes with five important qualities:

1. It's driven by the pursuit of growth (rather than the avoidance of pain).
2. It's grounded in healthy values (such as integrity, curiosity, compassion).
3. It is free of shame and fuelled by wanting the best for us (rather than fearing how other people might see you and fuelled by "not good enough").
4. The energy around the change is light. You feel uplifted, energized and optimistic when you think about making the change (rather than an urgent, heavy oh-my-god-everything-is-riding-on-this or I-need-this-to-happen-to-make-everything-better energy).
5. You take responsibility for your part in changing your life. You approach situations from a place of creator, rather than the place of a victim (we'll talk more about this dynamic in the next chapter).

Summary

In this chapter, we've looked at some key differences between change when the inner mentor is in control, and those driven by the inner critic. Both parts of you might want the same change, but the way they go about it and the energy behind it is very different. We've explored the apparent dichotomy between self-acceptance and a desire for change, and how a healthy desire for change is rooted in self-acceptance, not at odds with it. You've also learned about the key qualities of inner mentor-fuelled change and how you can use these to make changes in your life from a shame-free place of self-acceptance.

In the next chapter, I'll share more about how you can turn up the volume on your inner mentor and continue creating a deeper sense of harmony in your internal world.

Questions for Reflection

1. *Of the two types of motivation (motivation by fear or motivation by growth), which do you feel is more present in your life right now? How does this influence your self-talk?*
2. *What are your healthy values? If you'd like help with identifying these, you can get a free* Discover Your Values *workbook at:* http://bit.ly/discoveryourvalues
3. *Over the next week, make time each evening (even five minutes is enough) to check in with yourself and review any notable thoughts, feelings, reactions and decisions, from the day. Which do you think were dominated by your inner critic? And which by the inner mentor? How did the energy feel with each? Where did the feelings associated with each show up in your body? Do you notice any patterns?*

8

TURN UP THE VOLUME ON YOUR INNER MENTOR

Over the past few years, I've tried all the things to change my inner critic – some of which were much more successful than others. In developing a stronger connection with my inner mentor, I also experimented with ways of thinking about this internal voice, different ways of calling on it and different practices to put me in a good headspace to access this part of myself. In this chapter, I want to share some of the most useful tools and frameworks I've used with my inner mentor; I hope they are useful for you too.

As we've already explored, the presence of your inner critics themselves isn't a problem. What is a problem is the way they express themselves and the fact they can dominate your internal dialogue, drowning out any other parts of your inner chatter that might have more constructive and helpful thoughts and suggestions to offer you. As a part that helps you stay connected to your best self and keeps you in alignment with your values and priorities, the inner mentor can become lost in the noise and hard to hear. In the following pages, I will share a range of practical tools, journaling practices and thought exercises I've found helpful for strengthening my inner mentor and deepening my level of self-kindness in my daily life. Remember: self-kindness starts here and now, so you have permission to work through these suggestions at a pace that is invigorating without being overwhelming. As you go through this chapter, I encourage you to make a note of which of the ideas and practices resonate most with you and try these first before coming back to the others later.

Start in the Past

In the last chapter, I mentioned it's helpful to visualize what your inner mentor looks and sounds like. Visualization and role-playing are helpful for connecting with your inner mentor but using this powerful voice is necessary to strengthen it. To start, try doing this retrospectively once you notice your inner critic has taken charge. When you notice your inner critic has become your dominant inner voice, return to the questions from Chapter 2 about getting to know your inner critics. Trace them back to the source:

- When did your inner critic rear its head, what were you doing/saying/thinking about?
- What was the exact thought or memory that provoked that inner critic to speak up (and why?)
- What is your inner critic protecting or defending in its own way?

Take time to understand it. Then, visualize the inner

mentor figure you connected with in the previous chapter (and its qualities) and use it as a debriefing companion. What do you think your inner mentor would ask in this situation? What would they want to know about your critics, and what would they say in response?

Let's say you're feeling down and you realize that in the background of these feelings, your inner critic is haranguing you about your appearance: *You're frumpy, ungraceful, that person over there looks way better than you ever will,* etc. As soon as you notice this is happening, stop and use the tools from Part II to gain some emotional distance from your critic (remember: step away from the spiral of self-recrimination). Then, you can start to trace your thoughts back: when did this start? Who or what was the trigger? The size and shape of the trigger isn't necessarily proportional to the subsequent inner-critic attack. It could be as obvious as someone made a mean comment to you, but it could be as subtle as you saw someone laughing. It might have also been something you were thinking about from the past, or something you're worried about. Once you've identified the trigger point, you can call on your inner mentor to step in and take over. Your inner mentor might wonder what the message underneath the criticism is; perhaps you need a reminder of the values that matter most to you (regardless of what society's values seem to be). Or, perhaps you haven't been taking care of yourself, you want to, and this is what your inner critic is trying to tell you in its own way. Whatever the case is, you understand yourself and your critic better, and you can move forward with a calmer, more peaceful mind. You can also turn this into a regular practice as we'll explore with dialogues below.

Three Useful Journaling Practices

Journaling, as I've already mentioned in this book, is a useful way to get emotional distance and to process thoughts, feelings and experiences that are hard to make sense of in my head. Many journaling techniques are helpful for self-discovery, but I've found the following three techniques especially useful for turning up the volume on my inner mentor. Later in this chapter, you'll also find inner-mentor inspiring questions that make great springboards for journaling too.

Create a Character Sketch

In the last chapter, I mentioned the value of creating a visual image of your inner mentor, a figure or presence you can call to mind when you think of this part of yourself. This journaling tool gives you the chance to build on this visual image. To create a character sketch, describe your inner mentor in the way you would a character in a novel or a movie. As well as physical qualities – like appearance, age and gender – think about the emotional qualities they embody, the language they use and the principles that inform their wisdom and way of being. The more detail you can add to your mental image of your inner mentor's character, the better.

Questions to consider include:

- Who is your inner mentor?
- What does he or she look like?
- What is the quality and timbre of their voice?
- How do they hold themselves?

- Do they fit an archetype? If so, which one?
- What is the atmosphere like around them?

Visualizing your inner mentor for the first few times will work best when you are calm and relaxed. The first few times I tried this exercise, I was already feeling overwhelmed by my inner critics, and found it was almost impossible to connect with my inner mentor while I was in that head space. The more I practised accessing my inner mentor when I was in a peaceful state of mind, though, the easier it was to access this part of myself when I wasn't.

Dialogues

Dialogues involve writing out a conversation between two parts of your internal dialogue, as you would a script. You can choose whichever two parts you wish; for the purpose of this book, I'll be referring to a dialogue between your inner critic and inner mentor. In this situation, your inner mentor can function as a mediator, hosting a calm and respectful conversation between your inner critic and yourself.

Begin the conversation by asking your inner critic what it would like to say to you. Then, practise responding with your inner mentor, writing each response and line of dialogue as you go. In my experience, dialogues benefit my inner conversations in two ways.

First, as I've already mentioned, the act of writing things down gives me a different perspective on the things I'm writing about. While the thoughts and ideas exist just in my head, I'm often too close to the topic or thoughts to see them clearly. When I can write my thoughts and read them back, however, I'm looking at them from the outside and can see new perspectives, patterns and features I missed before. Second, writing this kind of conversation slows it down. This is especially helpful if, like me, your inner critic tends to dominate your internal dialogue.

Writing out the conversation like a script means I have to pause before each answer, which allows me to be more considered and respond rather than react. It also gives me the time to self-reflect in more depth as the conversation moves along and become more aware of the subtext and underlying thoughts and beliefs for each part. When I write dialogues, I have time to consciously connect to my inner mentor and imagine how she would respond. You can also use dialogues with any other parts of your internal dialogue that become triggered by your inner critics, such as the childlike part we explored in Chapter 1.

This exercise is particularly useful for the reflective practice I mentioned earlier in this chapter. Call to mind the figure you visualized in the previous chapter, as well as the qualities you'd like them to embody. Then, imagine what they would say, first in response to your inner critic and then in response to the situation that provoked your inner critic in the first place. The first few times you do this practice, it might feel stilted and unnatural. Your inner mentor's words might have no impact on your inner critic or how you're feeling.

I felt self-conscious the first few times I did this exercise (and noticed my inner critic was telling me this was a stupid idea and I looked like an idiot). But when I persisted and began to explore my critic's resistance to doing this exercise, I discovered it was afraid of change and afraid of becoming less powerful. This helped me understand it better, helped me take back the reins, and allowed my inner mentor to have a voice in the conversation too.

As I've already mentioned, my inner critics usually feel like they – and they alone – are responsible for my safety and wellbeing, which is a lot of pressure to shoulder. Practising dialogues helps relieve some of that pressure and creates a more peaceful coexistence between the different parts of my internal dialogue.

Write a Letter to Yourself

Write a letter to yourself from your inner mentor. You can do this about a certain situation, event or challenge you are facing in your life, or write a letter of general encouragement. You will find it easiest to do this if you set aside 30 minutes in a quiet place where you'll be uninterrupted. Relax as much as possible and use the inner mentor visualization questions from the previous chapter to bring this part of your inner dialogue to mind. Then, start writing. If you're not sure what to write, try asking your inner mentor questions like:

- What would you most like to tell me right now?
- What do you have to say about this situation?
- What advice do you have for me?
- What am I missing?
- What do you think my next step should be?

"One technique that has helped is to write myself letters.

When I am feeling very anxious I will write a letter to my 'calm' self. I will try to describe as precisely as possible how I am feeling physically and emotionally and why. I will describe what tools I have tried to use to help myself and whether they seem to be helping or not. At another time, when I am feeling calm and strong, I will write a letter to my 'anxious' self, explaining how it feels when I am able to look at things from the broader perspective, reminding myself that strong emotions pass with time, and giving explicit instructions for activities to help cope and/or distract. I find this conversation back and forth helps – at least sometimes!"

—Cynthia

Let it RAIN

The RAIN technique is a process that will help you shift from a place of self-criticism to a place of self-kindness. Each letter of this acronym describes a step you can take to counteract critical self-talk and consciously choose a more compassionate and loving internal dialogue. Originally developed by mindfulness teacher Michelle McDonald, psychologist Tara Brach describes this process in her essay for the book *The Self-Acceptance Project* in the following way:

R stands for recognize. This is the awareness we explored earlier in the book – using phrases: "I notice . . ." or "The story I'm telling myself is . . ." to name and give voice to my thoughts and feelings (see also Chapter 5). This step alone can provide some emotional distance and relief from the intensity of the feelings associated with my inner critics and their stories.

A stands for allow. You could also substitute "allow" for words like "acknowledge" or "accept". This step is about accepting how you feel and allowing yourself to feel it, no matter how uncomfortable it might feel to do so.

Accepting a feeling or thought doesn't mean you have to like it. Rather, this kind of acceptance is rooted in acknowledging reality and being able to say to yourself, "I am feeling [*insert emotion here*]," or "When my inner critic tells me I'm useless, I feel hopeless. The story I'm telling myself is there's no point in doing anything," and then allowing yourself to experience what that's like for a few moments. When I feel uncomfortable feelings or experience thoughts or stories I think are bad or wrong, it's tempting to try to push them down or change them as quickly as possible. But these feelings and thoughts are messages from my internal GPS. They are signposts to what is and isn't working in my life right now (even if it's that things are going well and sometimes it's hard to just enjoy being happy). When I try to change or push them away without accepting them first, they don't disappear. Instead, they are relegated to my unconscious, where they influence my feelings, thoughts and behaviour in ways I'm unaware of or don't understand.

Allowing, acknowledging and accepting your emotional experience enables you to be with your feelings so you can move on to the next step in the process.

I is for investigate. This is where your inner mentor steps up. Having recognized and accepted, now your inner mentor takes on the role of a compassionate inquirer, asking questions to further explore what's going on. I shared some of these questions earlier when we explored starting with the past, asking what triggered your inner critics and what you think is happening underneath its anger.

This step involves asking open questions rather than leading questions. When you ask leading questions, you already have a desired or "right" answer in mind and you ask questions that guide the conversation in a certain direction. Open questions, on the other hand, are as the name suggests – open to any answer and any direction. The point of this investigation isn't to convince yourself to change how you feel or to convince your inner critics they are wrong, but to get to the root of what's happening and explore how you'd like to respond.

N is for non-attachment. When I experience strong or overwhelming thoughts or feelings, it can also feel like they represent me as a person. As I discussed earlier, I've found it helpful to remember each of my inner critics is just one part of my internal dialogue. It might be a vocal, loud part, but it is just one aspect of my internal conversation. Non-attachment is about recognizing that I am not my thoughts and feelings. They are happening but they don't represent me as a person. When you recognize this, you can take on the role of an observer, noticing the stories you're telling yourself, without believing them or getting caught up in them.

In an article on the RAIN process published on the website *Psychology Today*, psychologist Meg Selig suggests adding "S" for "self-compassion" to this process.

S is for self-compassion. Again, this is a step for the inner mentor. Once you've recognized and acknowledged your feelings, investigated them and recognized they are part of you and happening inside you, but don't represent you as a whole, you can offer yourself self-compassion for your experience. For example, I might say to myself, "It's hard to hear what the inner critic has to say. It leaves me feeling powerless." Self-compassion isn't rooted in victimhood. It's not saying, "Poor me!" Instead, it's about witnessing and accepting. Self-compassion is showing myself the love, care and empathy I would show a loved one who is having a hard time.

A while ago, my husband and I were hosting a dinner party for two other couples. At one point I mentioned an incident that had happened to a family member of one of the couples, which I assumed was shared knowledge (couple one and two were good friends), but when couple two looked shocked and said, "X happened to [*family member*]?!" I realized I had just shared private information that wasn't mine to share.

"I'm really sorry," I blurted out to couple one, then to the others, "I thought you knew." They didn't. Couple one reassured me it was fine, and the conversation moved on but I spent the next 15 minutes squirming in my seat, replaying what I'd said repeatedly, and wishing I could disappear into a hole in the ground. *Of course that was private information, you idiot,* my inner critic was saying, *You think they will want to talk to you about anything now? Great job being a decent friend *slow clap*.*

This was when I let it RAIN. I recognized (R) the story I was telling myself was that I had screwed up. Couple one would think I was a gossip who didn't know how to handle personal information and would never trust me again. I had ruined the evening. I had damaged my husband's friendship with them too, and on and on. So I allowed (A). I let myself feel embarrassed. I recognized how much I wanted this evening to be a fun time with friends, and how I enjoyed and appreciated my friendship with couple one. I had made a mistake. I shouldn't have assumed the incident was common knowledge, and this was a valuable lesson for the future. Then, I investigated (I). Looking around, everyone else at the dinner party was relaxed, laughing, and enjoying themselves. No one had stormed out, no one had made their excuses and left, offended by my faux pas. Everyone had moved on and was having a great time – except me.

In this situation, non-attachment (N) looked like recognizing what my inner critic was saying wasn't necessarily true. And the situation wasn't irreparable. Then came self-compassion (S). Avoiding my mistake and hoping everything would be fine might have been more comfortable in the short term, but I would have felt terrible about it afterwards. In this situation, self-compassion looked like acknowledging I am human. Sometimes I speak without thinking. I make mistakes. But it also involved acknowledging my desire to make amends – even if my inner critic's harsh assessment of the situation made me want to bury my head in the sand and never mention it again. So, as everyone was leaving, I took couple one aside and apologized again, saying I shouldn't have assumed the other couple knew, it wasn't my information to share, and I was sorry. They were lovely about it and everything was fine, but even if it hadn't been, I knew speaking up to apologize again was the right thing to do in the situation.

Initially, you might find it easiest to work through these steps in writing (as I mentioned before, writing has the benefit of slowing everything down). Over time, however, you will become better at recognizing when you are feeling the effects of your inner critic and guiding yourself through this process with your inner mentor on your side.

Find Inner-Mentor Role Models

When I started connecting with, and strengthening my inner mentor, I didn't have a template for what a good inner mentor looked like, so I turned to the outside world to create one. Return to the list of inner mentor qualities you identified in the previous chapter. Now, think of people you know (or know of) who embody these qualities. How do they express them? How do they show up in the world? How do they talk about themselves?

You don't have to know these people in person. For example, you might choose someone whose blog, books, podcast or videos you read, listen to or follow, and whose presence resonates with you. It could also be someone who exudes one or more of these qualities in their public appearance. You also need not find one person who embodies all the qualities you'd like your inner mentor to have. Instead, cherry pick. You might know someone who has excellent boundaries and model that aspect of your inner mentor on her. You might also know someone else who exudes a level of self-confidence you'd love your inner mentor to embody and look at how they interact with the people and world around them. Some of my inner-mentor role models are people I know in person and who embody certain traits. Some are people I don't know, but who have had an influence on my life in other ways, for example authors like Brené Brown and Carl Rogers. I don't (and in the case of Carl Rogers won't) know them personally, but I can still immerse myself in their writing, internalize the ideas they talk about and adopt them as role models.

If you struggle with a vocal inner critic, especially if your inner critic leaves you feeling helpless and victimized, you might look to people who embody the qualities you would like to have yourself and feel a degree of comparison and inadequacy, even envy. Typically, these are seen as so-called bad experiences and emotions. While I don't think it's a good idea to believe the stories behind these feelings (nor act on them), I also don't agree with the assessment they are wrong, forbidden or feelings you or I should avoid.

Like all feelings, they are messages sharing something that needs attention within yourself or your life. And, as we've already explored in this book, you can listen to that message by noticing these feelings when they arise, allowing yourself to feel them, then becoming curious with yourself about what they represent and what's happening beneath the surface. As I talked about earlier in the book, when I compare myself negatively to others, it's usually because they are reflecting a quality or potential I'm not owning in myself. In this way, the people who trigger feelings of comparison, inadequacy or envy within you might in fact be the inner-mentor role models you are looking for. This isn't always the case (and I'm definitely not advocating placing emotional stock in people who leave you feeling bad about yourself), but it is worth exploring – especially if you struggle with comparison and "not good enough" feelings on a regular basis.

Use the 5 Per Cent Rule

A question I love and find helpful when I perceive the distance between where I am and where I'd like to be (or think I should be) is: *What would I do differently if I were 5 per cent kinder to myself today?*

Expecting myself to get to 100 per cent inner harmony, 100 per cent self-worth, or 0 per cent self-criticism overnight isn't realistic (or aligned with self-acceptance and self-compassion). But I can do 5 per cent, wherever I'm starting from – and so can you. You might not be able to envision what 100 per cent self-love or self-worth looks like, but you can imagine what it would look and feel like to raise your self-kindness game by 5 per cent. When you focus on the next 5 per cent, you can address each day as it comes, rather than feeling pressured to reach a finish line you can't even see.

When I started exploring my relationship with my inner critics, I was aiming to get to a point where I wouldn't experience self-criticism anymore. Needless to say, this left me feeling disappointed, frustrated and even worse about myself after every encounter with my critics, which I perceived as a setback. This pattern only changed when I learned about the 5 per cent rule from psychologist Nathaniel Branden, who encourages participants to reflect on this in his sentence completion exercises (you can find a link to these in the Resources at the back of the book). Upon reading this, something clicked. Instead of expecting myself to make dramatic shifts and change life-long patterns overnight, I started focusing on incremental changes. Rather than focusing on the fact I wasn't meeting this unrealistic goal I'd set for myself to never self-attack again, I noticed the times when I was making progress: experiencing 5 per cent more self-worth, being 5 per cent kinder to myself and inching up the scale. It's a much kinder way of thinking about change and has set me up for slow, sustainable growth, rather than striving based on expectations I can't meet. Make a practice of asking yourself: *If I were 5 per cent kinder to myself, what would I do differently today?*

Give Your Inner Mentor Evidence

I have found it's much easier to believe in myself when I have evidence to back up that belief – especially when my inner critics are so darn good at arguing with me! The purpose of creating counter-evidence isn't to enter into a debate with your inner critic (we all know how well that turns out). Instead, it's to provide fuel for the inner mentor. There are several kinds of inner mentor-strengthening evidence you can create, depending on what resonates for you.

> "My ideal relationship with myself is getting closer and closer to becoming reality. I have been shortening the time between when I first start hearing the inner critic and when I change the negative self-talk to positive. Ideally, I want this relationship to start from a place of positivity instead of changing from negative to positive. I'm practising that daily by writing one positive thing about myself in my journal every morning."
>
> —Mallory

As humans, we are natural problem-solvers and tend to devote more time and energy to focusing on potential problems and threats rather than our strengths and what's working. Focusing on my weaknesses, while part of my human wiring, gives my inner critic more ammunition and makes me more likely to miss valuable evidence that my inner mentor can use to encourage a more constructive internal dialogue. For a while, I noticed much of my journaling was focused on issues and problems. While expressing these things can be helpful, just exploring these aspects of my life was causing me to pay disproportionate attention to the negative while overlooking the positive.

One way I counterbalance this natural tendency is to keep a "three good things" journal. When I'm experiencing a challenging time, I have a practice of writing three good things at the end of each day. Everything I write becomes fodder for my inner mentor's responses to my inner critic and helps my mentor better support me. You can do the same, simply by keeping track of what is going well in your life. Whenever you have a positive experience, an accomplishment, something you feel proud of, a compliment or a pleasant surprise, write it down. I also keep a record of weekly "wins" in my journal: things I've accomplished, achieved, or feel proud of, and positive feedback and experiences from the last seven days. Things that go on these lists might include big events and accomplishments, but it's also important to write down the small wins from daily life too. Did you make a phone call you were feeling nervous about? Did you do something you've been putting off for ages? Did you speak up even when it felt hard? Win, win and win. Both of these practices are simple and take only a few minutes, but they both contribute to a growing body of evidence that perhaps I'm not as flawed as my inner critic makes me out to be.

Another practice I've found useful is starting my own "Secrets of Adulthood" list. This is an idea I borrowed from writer Gretchen Rubin, who shares more about this in her book, *The Happiness Project* and on her blog at gretchenrubin.com. These are lessons you've learned, epiphanies and wisdom you can relate to, and statements you know to be true for yourself or within your own life. Some of my own secrets of adulthood include:

- People are usually far too busy focusing on their own lives to spend as much time judging me as I worry they do.
- The next minute is always a chance to do something different.
- Assume the best.
- Do no harm but take no s***.
- When one door closes, another door opens.
- Choose integrity over comfort.

I find this list serves like a compass, pointing me back to what I've learned from my life experiences so far. Perhaps my perspective on these things will change, but for now revisiting these statements is a useful grounding exercise that helps clear any inner-critic-laden mental fog and reminds me of what's true and important in my life.

Use Inner-mentor Inspiring Questions

Your inner mentor functions as a combination of nurturer, guide and coach. To this end, you can strengthen this part of your internal dialogue by paying attention to the kinds of questions you ask yourself. As I mentioned when talking about the RAIN process, the most helpful questions are open, rather than closed. Here are a few inner-mentor-inspiring questions you can use to get started:

- Who do I want to become? Be mindful of not using your answer to criticize your present self implicitly. Rather than focusing on what you don't want to be or answering with "Less X", "More Y", focus on what you want to be with clear, concise statements. For example: confident, compassionate, courageous, etc.
- What qualities are most important for me to embody in my life? If you would like extra support with this, you can download a free workbook, *Discover Your Values,* from Becoming Who You Are, at http://bit.ly/discoveryourvalues – which will walk you through the process of identifying your core values and exploring how you can live them in your daily life.
- What experiences do I value most in my life? Why?
- What are my highest priorities?
- How are the traits I perceive as weaknesses also strengths?
- Why is this the perfect opportunity for me right now?

- What makes me a good person to be doing this?
- What are my strengths?
- What is the evidence I am becoming who I want to be?
- What if this works out exactly as I want it to? (This is a useful counter question to negative "what if?" questions.)
- What is my intuition saying about this?
- What is this situation teaching me?
- What are the opportunities in this situation?
- What do I want to create in this situation?
- What is my ideal outcome or resolution here?
- What would I tell my best friend in this situation?
- If I were 5 per cent kinder to myself, what would I tell myself right now?
- If I were to bring the best version of myself to this situation, how would I show up?
- What am I needing right now? And how can I meet those needs?

The more you use these questions, the more you will internalize them and the more they will become a natural part of your internal dialogue. As you strengthen your inner mentor, you will encounter other questions on your journey that you'll find helpful or resonate. Make a note of them and review them regularly. You can use these inner-mentor inspiring questions as and when you need to; or make a practice of selecting five-or-so questions to ask yourself each morning.

Therapy can be an invaluable tool, especially if you're struggling to connect with your inner mentor, suspect or know you need support to heal from past experiences or abuse, or are feeling overwhelmed by your inner critics. An important part of self-kindness is being aware of and acknowledging when you need some additional support, then taking steps to get that support.

I use the terms counselling and therapy interchangeably (if you're interested in the difference, I've included a link to an article on this topic in the Resources at the back of this book). While I am not a licenced counsellor or therapist, I have experienced over six years of therapy and counselling as a client, with different therapists and a variety of experiences (good and bad), plus a year's training as a counsellor. Here are few guideposts I've found helpful when looking for a therapist or counsellor.

1. Appropriate training: Find a good, qualified therapist. Training is important as it increases the likelihood (although doesn't guarantee it) that they can hold space for you and separate out as much as possible their own thoughts and feelings from yours. However, the rapport you have with a potential counsellor is more important than the level of training they've had. Someone with a PHD in counselling psychology isn't necessarily going to be a better person for you than someone with a one- or two-year diploma if you can't relate to them on a personal level and feel a sense of connection.

2. Self-awareness and self-acceptance: This, along with the ability to hold space for difficult issues and challenges, is why training is so important. Good therapy training comes with a large component of self-reflection on the part of the counsellor or therapist and ideally continues through supervision while they are working with clients. Good therapists should strive as much as possible to know of their own blind spots, trigger points, beliefs and conditioning, so they can be present, reflective and accepting of their clients.

3. Good listening and reflection skills: This sounds obvious but good listening and reflection skills are not always a given, even though they are so important. You'll know if someone has these skills because you'll feel seen and listened to. Your therapist might even show as much by reflecting what they've heard and understood.

4. Acceptance of and empathy for you: We all have our judgements and prejudices, but a good therapist will be aware of theirs and will be able compartmentalize them, holding space for you to explore your beliefs without forcing theirs on you. The point of therapy is for you to explore who *you* are. While therapists might share opinions when they believe it serves your growth, they should do so in the context of accepting and empathizing with your experiences too.

5. A willingness to work with you for your growth: There is a difference between working with you on the level of adding you to their client list and working with you as part of a therapeutic alliance and partnership. You want a sense your therapist will actively work with you and go wherever you go during your sessions. This doesn't mean they will do the work for you, but they also won't leave you out in the cold with certain topics or difficult discussions.

6. Boundaries: The therapeutic relationship is unlike any other; it isn't friendship, nor familial, nor romantic. Your therapist might come to know you better than most other people in your life – possibly anyone. At the same time, you won't know a great deal about them, beyond what they share. You are not there to take care of your therapist's feelings or to be their friend. Strong boundaries are crucial to the therapeutic relationship because they are a large part of what makes it feel safe.

7. Someone you feel comfortable with: It's often hard to put a finger on exactly why you might or might not feel comfortable with someone. It might be their demeanour, something they say, their presence in the room, the way they make eye contact, their facial expressions, or a myriad of other things personal to you. Trust is a huge part of the relationship – you need to know your therapist is trustworthy, not only in terms of confidentiality but also in the way they will receive what you share. And this starts with you feeling comfortable with them. Intuition is important here. When you don't feel comfortable with someone, it's often because you are picking up on one or more red flags, or because you don't gel with them on an individual level. At the beginning of every therapeutic relationship, there is a level of adjustment, testing the waters and getting comfortable opening up, but I've found I've known within the first session or two whether I will have a positive experience or not.

Therapy isn't essential for developing a kinder relationship with yourself, but it can be invaluable for helping you turn up the volume on your inner mentor. This is especially the case if you often feel overwhelmed by self-criticism or you're finding it challenging to access your inner mentor on your own. Therapy can also be helpful if you find you become flooded with strong feelings while working through the practices and feel you would benefit from support while doing so. You know yourself best and an important aspect of self-kindness is giving yourself the support you need.

> "If we can share our story with someone who responds with empathy and understanding, shame can't survive."
>
> —Brené Brown, *Daring Greatly: How the Courage to Be Vulnerable Transforms the Way We Live, Love, Parent, and Lead*

The Inner-Mentor Mindset

If you've been around the personal growth space any amount of time, you'll know mindset is important, but what does this look like in the context of your inner mentor? In the rest of this chapter, I want to share two mindset shifts that have helped me strengthen my inner mentor: a growth mindset and the creator orientation.

Embracing a Growth Mindset

As I mentioned above, the purpose of the inner mentor is to act as a leader and mediator, sharing wisdom, experience, intuition and – when needed – a different perspective. The inner mentor's role is not to always cheer you on. Sometimes, you will do things that don't warrant cheerleading but are most kindly responded to with accountability and a reminder to recommit to your values. You inner mentor is there to guide you through these times with care and compassion.

In this way, inner mentors encourage what psychologist Carol Dweck refers to as a growth mindset. She defines this way of thinking as a set of beliefs around your potential. People with a growth mindset believe they can change and develop themselves, their skills and talents through hard work, useful feedback and a strategic approach to progress. With a work project, this might look like recognizing the areas where you're not performing as well as you'd like to; and enlisting the support and training you need to improve – recognizing that improvement is possible with practise and the right tools. Returning to the subject of this book, a growth mindset around self-kindness might look like recognizing the situations in which you struggle with your inner critic and figuring out what will be most helpful for creating a more constructive internal dialogue. With a growth mindset, you recognize success is mostly due to hard work (rather than innate intelligence or talent) and view challenges and setbacks as opportunities for learning and growth.

If you have a fixed mindset, on the other hand, you believe traits like talent and intelligence are set in stone. You either have them or you don't. People with this mindset also believe that success is largely due to these traits and they are fixed from birth. This means they are more focused on *looking* smart or accomplished, rather than actually *becoming* these things. This mindset can lead to them avoiding risks, giving up easily, viewing effort as a waste of time, and feeling threatened by the success of others. Someone with this mindset believes if you can't do something perfectly from the get go, there's no point in even trying. Sound familiar? That's because the fixed mindset is the domain of the inner critic (while, as I just described, a growth mindset is encouraged by the inner mentor).

You can strengthen your inner mentor by practising switching any fixed mindset thoughts for those more aligned with a growth mindset as soon as you recognize them. Not only will this help you turn down the volume on your inner critic and turn up the volume on your inner mentor, but it will also help you become more resilient, open to trying new things, and give you a greater sense of free will. For a much more detailed exploration of fixed mindset and growth mindset, I recommend reading *Mindset* by Carol Dweck and *The Pursuit of Perfect* by Tal Ben-Shahar.

Living as a Creator, Not as a Victim

I've already talked about how my inner critics can provoke another part of my internal dialogue that feels helpless and victimized, which is why the mindset shift I'm going to describe next resonated with my experience of the world – and myself. My a-ha moment came when I truly understood that how I relate to the world around me is both influenced by, and reinforces, my relationship with myself. One example of this is the social model of "The Drama Triangle", which was originally conceived by Dr. Stephen Karpman. The Drama Triangle is dynamic, a specific way of relating to the world, which revolves around three interchangeable roles you can take in any given interaction. These three roles are: victim, persecutor and rescuer. I'll explain these roles, plus show how they relate to your relationship with you and your inner critics, and then share the alternative: "The Empowerment Dynamic". This is a framework laid out by David Emerald in his book *The Power of TED* (*The Empowerment Dynamic)*. Although he applies this dynamic to external situations – such as our relationships with others and how we cope with life's ups and downs – I found the principles and mindsets within the Empowerment Dynamic to be just as relevant and invaluable for my relationship with myself, my inner critic and my inner mentor too. For a visual representation of the models in this section, please visit www.powerofted.com.

As the name suggests, each role within the Drama Triangle inhabits a point on a triangle. The victim is the primary role. The victim feels like things happen to them that are largely out of their control, which leaves them feeling helpless and disempowered. As Emerald points out, all victims have experienced a loss in the form of a thwarted dream or desire, whether that's to do with health, identity or even their sense of reality (for example, if they believe they are happily married but then discover their spouse is having an affair). The Drama Triangle isn't about whether you experience upsets – everyone does to greater and lesser degrees. What propels you into a victim *role*, however, is how you *relate* to the experiences or events that happen. Victims are reactionary and tend to have a default knee-jerk response that keeps them stuck in victimhood. With your inner critic, you – or that child-like part of your internal dialogue – might feel like a victim of its attacks.

Moving to the lower right point on the triangle, the

persecutor can be a person, a situation or an event. It might be a family member, a spouse, an illness or an event, like bankruptcy, an earthquake or any other happening involving challenge or hardship. The persecutor is the perceived cause of the victim's woes. I say perceived because the victim might view the persecutor as the source of their hardship and misery but that doesn't mean it's true. Genuine persecutors do exist, however. If someone is entrenched in the Drama Triangle, they might oscillate between victim, persecutor and saviour within their interpersonal relationships. When I think back to times I was reacting from within the Drama Triangle, my inner critic felt like a persecutor – blaming, shaming, and criticizing me to control me and keep me small.

The final piece of the Drama Triangle is the rescuer (also called the saviour). The rescuer intervenes on behalf of the victim, as the name suggests, trying to rescue them from the persecutor. Like the persecutor, the rescuer can be a person or it can be a situation or event, such as winning the lottery, or even something like an addiction, which makes you "feel better" in the short term. This role is tricky because it might not seem like there's anything wrong with being a rescuer. However, in person form, rescuers often are motivated to rescue because they would feel guilty not doing so. They also reinforce the victim's feelings of pity and, by trying to fix things, leave them feeling more disempowered, helpless and dependent. In the context of my inner critics, I can see examples of how I've looked to a "rescuer" for approval or validation in the belief if I get enough of that approval and validation, it will make my critics disappear. I've also used external accomplishments, achievements and desired states (e.g. getting a promotion, reaching a certain weight or earning a certain amount of money) as potential rescuers. I've told myself when I reach or attain that particular accomplishment, achievement or state, then my inner critics will be silenced for good. Needless to say, this doesn't happen. Even when I've reached those points, my inner critics have moved on to something new. Now, "when . . . then . . ." thinking is a red flag I'm back in the Drama Triangle, looking for the one thing that will rescue me, and need to shift my thinking toward the alternative I'll describe next.

If you recognize you're stuck in the Drama Triangle with your inner critics, what can you do? David Emerald shares an alternative way of relating to the world that, in my experience, works just as well with my inner critics too. It's called the "Empowerment Dynamic" and it helped me to break the cycle of feeling like the helpless victim of my inner critics and regain control. This enabled me to work with my inner mentor rather than feel controlled and at the mercy of my inner critics.

In the Empowerment Dynamic, the three roles I've just described, and the dynamics between them, change. The main role of victim becomes the main role of *creator*. A creator knows the ideal outcome he or she would like, and uses passion and intention to take clear, considered action toward that outcome. They choose their response to a situation, rather than being driven by reactionary emotions and behaviour, and remain focused on their vision. The persecutor becomes the *challenger*. Rather than being invested in keeping the primary role small, like the persecutor, the challenger's role is to call forth the creator's will to create. A challenger might encourage a creator to learn new skills, make difficult decisions and do what's necessary to manifest a dream or desire. Like the persecutor, the challenger can be a person, event or situation.

The role of challenger manifests in my inner dialogue in two ways. The first involves the inner mentor who is a *constructive challenger*. She offers the feedback I need to grow and become the best version of myself I can be. Dealing with my inner mentor isn't always easy. She can dish out some uncomfortable truths. But I know she has my best interests at heart. Recognizing my inner critics as *destructive challengers,* those that encourage me to face something difficult within myself, has also helped me develop a greater sense of agency and empowerment, without needing my critics to change or disappear. As I've already mentioned, these dynamics are not so much about what happens, but how I *relate and respond* to what happens. So I have a choice: either I can view my inner critic as a persecutor – and myself as a powerless victim – or I can see it as a destructive challenger, one that forces me to examine my relationship with myself and learn from my experiences. However painful or difficult your relationship with your inner critic has been to this point, you can use the pain and difficulty to mine for gold and create the internal peace, harmony and strength you crave.

Finally, the rescuer becomes the *coach*. While the rescuer tries to fix or solve things for the victim, the coach sees other people as creators of their own destiny. They facilitate personal progress and offer support, but they offer that support by standing by someone else rather than saying "let me fix it for you" or "let me fix you", which is the subtext of the rescuer. The inner mentor also plays the role of coach within your internal dialogue.

So how can you shift your relationship with these parts of your inner dialogue from a victim orientation to a creator orientation? Start by noticing the choices you make regarding how you respond to people, situations and events in life – including how you respond to the different parts of your internal dialogue. What are the stories you believe without questioning? What assumptions do you make about yourself and the world? Where are you adopting the role of victim, and where you taking on the role of creator? How do you talk about yourself and your life? How do you think about and approach your relationship with yourself, and particularly your inner critics?

According to Emerald, the three key shifts that can help us move from victim to creator form the acronym AIR, which stands for *Attention*, *Intention* and *Results*.

The first step, Attention, involves a shift in focus. When we're in the victim orientation, we tend to focus on our problems. Creators, on the other hand, focus on their vision and what they want to create. Within the context of my inner critics, this means I can focus on how nasty my critics are, and how I could only do X, Y and Z if they weren't so vocal, or I can ask myself questions like, *What do I* ***want*** *my relationship with my inner critic to be like? I've heard from my inner critics, now I wonder what my inner mentor would have to say about this?* With both sets of questions, I'm addressing the same thing – my inner critic – but I'm doing so from two very different angles, which lead to very different results.

The second step, Intention, is about motivation. While victims are motivated by wanting to get away from problems and act to alleviate their anxiety around those problems, creators are motivated by wanting to turn their vision into real-life outcomes (remember how we talked about the difference between avoiding pain and seeking growth in the last chapter?). In basic terms, they focus on they want, rather than on what they don't. So I have a choice: I can view this process as wanting to get rid of my inner critic so I can get on with my life in peace (an attitude that gives the inner critic a lot of power and puts me in the position of helpless victim); or, I can focus on strengthening my inner mentor, living as the best version of myself I can be each day and giving myself the best chance of making the most out of my life. When I look at my internal dialogue this way, it doesn't matter what my inner critic does or doesn't do. Instead of focusing on relieving pain, I'm focus on promoting strength and growth. This is a subtle difference, but it is important.

The third step, Results, is about the outcome of our attention and intention. When we're in a victim orientation, we usually go for immediate, short-term results. Once we no longer feel anxious about the problem at hand, we stop taking action – even if we haven't solved the problem itself. This is when we usually try to shut our inner critic up, call it names or silence it in other ways because we're trying to ease our immediate discomfort, but we're not getting to the root of the problem. This is when we need to ask: "Why is my inner critic so vocal in the first place? Why is it so passionate about what it's trying to say?" If you approach your critics in the creator orientation, however, you will take sustainable baby steps and focus on pursuing long-lasting results rather than short-term comfort.

Living life from a creator orientation doesn't mean you'll never experience anxiety or discomfort (nor does it mean you'll never hear from your inner critics again). Instead, it's about how you respond to your critics and the choices you make in the face of that discomfort and anxiety.

Summary

In this chapter, I've shared some techniques that can be helpful in turning up the volume on your inner mentor. As well as practical steps, like journaling and therapy, and how your mindset can create a shift from being dominated by your inner critics to working in partnership with your inner mentor. Noticing when you're using a fixed mindset rather than a growth mindset will help you be more mindful about when you're adopting the beliefs of the inner critic and help you consciously think more like your inner mentors. At the same time, paying attention to how you relate to your inner critic – as a victim or a creator – gives you the power to redefine your relationship with your critics without needing them to change at all. This transforms you from being beholden to your inner critics to reclaiming your power and control over your life.

In the next chapter, I'll share more about how the inner mentor and the inner critics can work together to not only create a more harmonious internal relationship but also to help you further your ambitions, goals and dreams for a life fully lived.

Questions for Reflection

1. *In which areas of your life have you been working with a fixed mindset? How has your inner critic influenced this? What would it look like to shift to a growth mindset in these areas? How would you talk to yourself if you had a growth mindset? How would you approach challenges, obstacles and successes? How would you feel differently about this area of your life?*
2. *Practise using AIR with your inner critics. Start by thinking about a recent time you experienced one or more of your critics becoming vocal. What would you have done differently, if you had used the AIR framework? How would you have responded? How would you have felt? As you develop a more mindful relationship with your inner critics, experiment with using this practice in real time.*
3. *Start a regular journaling practice, using the prompts I've shared in this chapter and return to them regularly to practise reconnecting with your inner mentor.*

9

MENTOR AND CRITIC: A SUPERHERO DUO

After years of trying to shut up my inner critic, drown it out and ignore it, learning to empathize with it and recognizing I didn't need to wait for it to disappear to get on with my life was a revelation. Not only that, but I realized that in certain situations my inner critic is useful. In the right context, with the right boundaries, and without letting my inner critic take the reins, it can still give me valuable feedback I can use to be the best version of myself. In this chapter, I want to share more about situations in which your inner critics can be allies and how to take their feedback with a balanced perspective – knowing the difference between the times when disengaging is the best course of action and the times when you might want to take their points on board.

As I've already explained, an important part of self-kindness is accepting, and showing compassion to, all aspects of yourself. This includes your inner critic. Self-kindness is not just about being nice to yourself; it also involves being able to face difficult truths, share constructive feedback with yourself, and support your growth and development. This isn't always easy or comfortable.

I've also explained one reason you don't want to banish or shut down your critics altogether is because, in the right circumstances, they can be useful. When you are doing your most important, courageous work, when you are taking a risk, or when you are doing something that propels you out of your comfort zone into, as the saying goes, "where the magic happens" – this is when your inner critics will speak up. This doesn't mean every time your inner critics appear it's because you're doing something amazing (mine are vocal when I'm doing something that's the opposite of amazing too!), but when you do something that takes you above and beyond your normal ways of living, you can almost guarantee they will appear. This applies to all corners of life, from embarking on a new job or challenging work project to starting a new relationship, taking up a new hobby, or moving to a new place.

In this chapter, you'll discover more about when and how your critics can help you, and how you can use them with the inner mentor to make the most of your talents, expand your skillset, deepen your creativity and grow.

When Your Inner Critics Aren't Helpful

In previous chapters, we've explored the underlying messages, beliefs and fears of your inner critics – using tools like dialogues and questioning. Now, let's examine when you might want to listen to those messages, when you might want to say, "Thank you for sharing" and let that message go, and how to know the difference between the times to listen and the times to let go.

At this stage, you are probably much more familiar with the times that your inner critics are *not* useful, so let's start there. Here is a non-exhaustive list of situations in which you can listen to then let go of your inner critic's messages, using some of the techniques I've shared in this book:

When Your Inner Critics Are Name-calling

We've already talked about setting boundaries with your inner critic and using phrases like "I notice . . ." and "The story I'm telling myself is . . ." to get emotional distance from your critics' claims about you. While it is useful to dig down to acknowledge and explore the fear or belief underneath these exhortations, you don't want to listen to, or internalize, trash talk. A good rule of thumb is: if it's something you wouldn't say to a child/your best friend, it's not helpful dialogue to have with yourself.

When You're Doing Something for Fun

You might be familiar with the scene: you start a new hobby, one you've been looking forward to for months. Initially, it's fun. Then your inner critic pipes up: *You're not very good at this, are you? Why bother?* and the usual chatter from the peanut gallery begins. If you struggle with a perfectionist critic, it's hard to do things for fun. Activities you undertake for enjoyment soon become a heated competition, if not against other people then with yourself. Soon, your activity starts feeling less joyful and more jarring. Instead of looking forward to it, it becomes framed with a sense of dread and "not good enough".

Fun needs to be just that: fun. My inner critics might have their opinions about the way I spend my leisure time, the hobbies I pursue and the things that bring me enjoyment, but they can have their opinions and I can still have my joy. If you find your inner critic persists in trying to interrupt your fun, you might find it helpful to explore whether there are limiting beliefs fuelling its attacks. Questions to explore include:

- What do I think about fun? What kind of role do I believe it should have in my life?
- When is fun okay? And when is it not okay?
- What do I believe is the "right" way to have fun? Why is that?
- What are my critic's fears and beliefs about me having fun? What is it worried about? Why else might it be trying to stop me?

You can add your own questions to this list too.

When You're Just Getting Started

Similar to having fun, this scenario tends to bring out any perfectionist critics that might be waiting for an opportunity to pipe up. Wedded to a fixed mindset, this critic buys into the belief that if you're not good at something from day one, there's no point in even trying.

As you know by now, this isn't true. If you notice your critic pops up to critique your lack of ability when you try something new (even if it's a skill you need to develop or something you want to become good at), this is a great opportunity to practise adopting the growth mindset of the inner mentor. I find it helpful to remind myself of simple truths, like, "The more time I spend on this, the better I'll become at it" or "Everybody starts as a beginner". If I'm doing something with a tangible output (for example, writing), I keep a record of my progress and how often I've practised. This way, during those times I feel impatient to improve, or am tempted to quit prematurely, I can remind myself of how far I've already come and how much effort I'm putting in (which is the one thing I have control over).

In dealing with my perfectionist critic, I also find it helpful to set aside a specific amount of time to play around: to doodle, to brainstorm and experiment with no expectations or outcomes in mind. Rather than diving straight in and expecting myself to make linear progress from the get go, I practise giving myself space to play before I "officially" begin. If it's still hard to distance yourself from a persistent critic, and if the following option is possible, try moving to somewhere you don't usually do that activity and continue your experimentation there. Often, a change of scene can help me change my thought patterns and get out of a particular critic rut.

When You're Dealing with a Situation That Requires Mindfulness, Attention and/or Responsiveness

One of the most debilitating effects of my inner critics is paralysis (remember the inaction I mentioned in Chapter 3?). A well-aimed inner critic barb can stop me in my tracks and leave me feeling disorientated, unsure of my next move, and unable to see north from south, in order to keep going. I find I can become so caught up in my critic's stories that I become tangled in my thoughts, inward facing at the expense of noticing and engaged with what's going on outside.

When I'm in a situation that requires mindfulness, attention and/or responsiveness, getting caught up in self-recrimination prevents me being present and taking necessary action. Using a situation that's happened to me before, as an example, let's say a friend is having a crisis and is asking me for support. I try to comfort her, only for my inner critic to pipe up: *Why did you say that? What a stupid thing to say – and after she turned to you for support. What kind of friend are you...?* But by the time I've had these thoughts, I've missed what my friend has been saying and have lost track of the conversation.

As I mentioned in Chapter 3, the irony of having a vocal and controlling inner critic is that by becoming involved in my inner critic's stories about how I'm not being supportive, I am less supportive. Instead of being present, engaged and listening, I become inward focused and preoccupied with my inner chatter. A similar catch-22 situation has come up when I've been in a new social situation or meeting someone for the first time. On these occasions, I've become so preoccupied with wondering what they think of me that I'm not present and therefore less likely to connect with them in the way I would like. The quickest way to stop this cycle is to be as aware as possible of where my attention is and bring it back to the present as soon as I notice I'm getting caught up in my thoughts.

This is something you can practise on your own that will then translate into your daily life. If you know you struggle to stay present in situations because of your inner critic, try sitting for 10 minutes every morning simply observing your thoughts and feelings. The way I like to do this is to sit in a chair or cross-legged, soften my gaze, and focus on a single point a few feet in front of me. As soon as I notice I'm caught up in a train of thought, I shift my focus back to whatever it is I'm looking at. This point becomes an anchor I can return to whenever I notice my attention has wandered. Other potential anchors are your breathing, focusing on the sensation of your chest rising and falling as you inhale and exhale, and any physical sensations you experience – such as the feeling of the air on your skin, the temperature, the touch of your clothes and so on. The focal point you choose is up to you, what matters most is it's something you can shift your attention back to whenever you notice you're engaging with your thoughts instead.

This practice is simple but not easy! The more you practise cultivating this kind of awareness and attention, however, the more you can take that awareness and attention into your interactions with the wider world. As you become more adept at noticing and shifting your focus when it strays, the easier this will be to do out in the real world too.

When Your Critics Overwhelm You

If your critics become too overwhelming, you can experience what is called "psychological flooding". This is when your nervous system becomes so overwhelmed that you cannot think clearly, make rational decisions or communicate effectively. For me, flooding feels like a physical wave of strong emotion running through my body. Some people also describe it as being like a punch in the gut.

This intense emotional experience isn't helpful as it leads to the fight, flight, freeze, submit response (see also Chapter 2). When I realize I'm in this place, the first thing I do is try to calm myself and my nervous system. Although it sounds simple – perhaps too simple to work – shifting my attention to my breath and taking long, deep breaths can be very effective. I breathe this way until I feel myself coming back into my body. Then, I encourage my critics to tell me more, not in the way they've just been speaking but on my terms. Instead of listening to what I'm doing wrong, what's not good enough, and the usual chatter, I ask questions:

- So what do you think I should do?
- What specifically do I need to improve here?
- How do you think I should approach this differently?
- What would that look like in practice?

Asking these questions helps me move beyond any hurtful and unconstructive dialogue and brings the different parts of my internal dialogue together to focus on a common goal: growth.

Learning to Put Your Inner Critic to Constructive Use

Having explored some of the situations in which your inner critics aren't helpful, now let's turn to some of the situations in which they are. Depending on your current experience of your inner critics, it might not feel like you can use them for good right now, but you can – especially alongside your inner mentor. Remember: their current form of communication might be more helpful rather than hurtful, but their underlying messages can contain gold. I have found behind the harsh words, there is sometimes a grain of truth and something I can learn from and improve. My inner mentor might be better at communicating this, but the inner critic is responsible for the ideas. Transforming your inner critics' voices from hurtful and undermining to constructive won't happen overnight, but the more you practise the exercises and reflective practices in this book, the more natural this new way of relating to yourself will become. Here are a few situations in which you can use your inner critics to further support your growth:

When You Want to Improve

Although your inner critics are not helpful when you're starting out with something new, they can be useful when you want to improve a skill, project or area of life. In this context, a toned-down inner critic's observations, filtered through your inner mentor, can be helpful – especially used with the questions I shared above, "When Your Critics Overwhelm You". They can point out specific ways you can improve, highlight the things you need to focus on to better your skills and yourself, and point out potential risks and stumbling blocks along the way. The key difference between this kind of constructive criticism and the destructive criticism you probably know all too well is the *intention*. Constructive criticism is rooted in the desire to grow and improve, destructive criticism is borne out of feeling the need to shrink down and stay hidden. If your inner critic is telling you all the reasons why you shouldn't do something full stop, ask yourself whether that something is dangerous, goes against your values, or conflicts with your other goals. If not, that is a sign your inner critic is offering destructive criticism (and, if it conflicts with any of those things, perhaps you need to revisit your idea). Asking questions like, *Am I avoiding pain or seeking growth? and Is this internal chatter motivated by fear or by love?* can help you stay mindful of which kind of criticism you're encountering.

When Your Performance or Work Is Under Judgement

Just as your inner critics can be useful when you want to work at improving a skill or aspect of your life, they can also be useful when you're in a situation where your performance or work is under some kind of judgement or where you want to persuade someone. Examples of this might be entering a competition, selling your work or services, applying for a new job or asking for a raise. In these situations, your inner critics can help you see your work or performance through the eyes of whoever is on the other side of the interaction, whether that be the judge, the client, your boss, etc.

Paired with your ability to empathize with the other side's experience, in this situation your critics and inner mentor can offer helpful feedback and advise how you can improve what you're offering and the way you're communicating that. This is especially helpful if your performance has a direct effect on your future wellbeing (for example, applying for a new job).

As you now know, it's important that your critics stick to constructive criticism. In these situations, destructive criticism is likely to leave you feeling paralysed and unable to communicate or perform to the best of your abilities. Constructive criticism, on the other hand, can help you identify how you can better highlight your value to a potential employer or boss, how to create the best product or service for a client and so on. It's also important to adopt a growth mindset in this realm. The critic's observations aren't a sign you shouldn't do it, just markers of where you can improve.

When You Make a Mistake or Lack Integrity

As much I try to live in alignment with my values, act with integrity and be a good person, I'm fallible and I do screw up. Rather than holding myself to impossible standards, I can use these inevitable times of discomfort, embarrassment and regret to live and learn. Left to run wild, my inner critics can turn these moments into spirals of shame, leaving me paralysed and more likely to avoid the situation than to make amends because I feel so awful about it (and myself) But, with my inner critics and inner mentor working together, I can use these situations to reflect, grow, make amends and hopefully do differently next time.

Summary

At this point, you have a better idea of what your inner critics are, where they come from, their purpose and intentions, and how to work with your inner mentor to transform them from a destructive force to a constructive force. This is where your journey truly begins. Like all relationships, your relationship with yourself will take maintenance. It requires you to show up each day, to demonstrate presence, attentiveness, patience, understanding and all the other qualities that lend themselves to harmony in your external relationships.

Just like external relationships, you will also have stumbling points and setbacks. I experience days when I feel like I'm done with my inner critics and don't want to deal with them any more (for better or for worse, however, unlike an external relationship, I can't leave my inner critics). If you're like me, you'll also experience days when you have the same discussions with your inner critic over the same sticking points – repeatedly – and you'll wonder whether things will ever get better. But in between these times, you'll also have moments where you notice things are calmer and your mind is more peaceful. You'll face a challenge, or a trying time, and notice how much better you're working with yourself (rather than despite or against yourself). You'll look back one day and realize this is the longest period you've gone without a full-scale inner-critic onslaught you can remember. Like relationships where each party has forgotten how to connect, you'll experience a mix of highs and lows as you learn how to re-join the same path together.

> "To me, this is an ongoing growth that will continue for the rest of my life. So what will be different from today will be that I will be further along on this journey every day. Setbacks will come. Life will throw me new curve balls. Hopefully I will handle each new one consciously and confidently."
>
> —Angie

Like external relationships old habits die hard– and old dynamics do too. Remember the neural pathways I described in the last chapter? The deeper and more entrenched those pathways are, the more patience and persistence you'll need to change them. Even though your inner critics aren't pleasant to deal with, if they are what you've known for decades, they are what you know. As much as you might desire a life with inner harmony rather than inner discord, it can feel alien to experience that life at first. Just as things are changing, that's when you're most likely to return to your old patterns and the comfortable familiarity they bring. Any change – and especially one that affects something so key as your relationship with yourself – requires a willingness to leap into the unknown, the patience to sit with the discomfort of uncertainty, and the courage to be open to what comes next.

As I hope is clear by now, the point of this work isn't to get rid of your inner critic but to change the way you relate to it. Your inner critics might not change – I hope over time they will learn to express themselves more constructively – but the only thing you can change is how you respond and what you do next when they speak up.

The choice is yours. It's time to step out of what you've known and embrace all you are and have yet to become.

> "Don't give up! Changing your attitude toward yourself is going to take time and work – you are undoing years (in my case a lifetime) of negative self-talk. It's not going to happen overnight, but the more you practise self-kindness the easier it will become."
>
> —Mallory

Questions for Reflection

1. *In which situations are your critics most likely to appear? How do you want to respond to them in those situations? How do you think changing your response would alter how you feel about those situations? What would change in your life as a result?*
2. *In which situations do you think your critics (working alongside your inner mentor) could be most helpful in your life?*
3. *How would you like to approach these situations going forward, so you can enjoy a constructive collaboration between your inner mentor and your inner critics?*

CONCLUSION

YOUR SELF-KINDNESS JOURNEY STARTS HERE

Thanks for reading. I hope you've enjoyed this book, and it's given you an insight into how you can redefine your relationship with your inner critic, turn up the volume on your inner mentor, and all the tools and resources you need to help you on your journey. If you enjoyed this book, I'd be grateful if you could take a moment to leave a review on Amazon or the website where you purchased your copy. Sharing your thoughts helps other readers learn more about the book and helps me improve as an author.

Learning to live with your inner critic isn't easy, and it can sometimes feel like one step forward, two steps back. Celebrate the good days and the small wins – when you encounter a challenging situation and afterwards realize you responded fairly and kindly toward yourself, when your inner critic pipes up and you're able to take back control of your internal dialogue in a firm but compassionate way, and all the other moment-to-moment instances you'll notice over the coming months.

On the not-so-good days, I invite you to return to a few basic facts about your inner critic:

- Your inner critic evolved to keep you in line with the values, beliefs and scripts with which you were raised.
- Your inner critic is trying to protect you (even though this can be hard to see at times). It truly believes it's working for your best interests and it wants the best for you – it just doesn't know when to stop.
- Transforming your relationship with your inner critic isn't about crushing it, ignoring it or trying to will it away. Self-compassion means accepting and empathizing with all parts of yourself, not just the comfortable or so-called positive parts. Over time, acknowledging, accepting and taking ownership over all parts of your internal dialogue – and especially turning up the volume on your inner mentor – will help your inner critic work with you, rather than against you.

Of course, reading a book about transforming your relationship with your inner critics is just the beginning. I'm great at reading personal growth books but putting the ideas into action is another process altogether! The biggest, and most important, part of this book is taking action: answering the reflective questions – if you haven't done so already and putting the ideas in into practice. By taking the time to read these chapters, you've already shown yourself your wellbeing is important and self-kindness matters to you. My hope for you is that you can continue this practice from here.

If you'd like additional resources for your journey, I invite you to enjoy a free video class on self-kindness. Simply go to http://selfkindness.becomingwhoyouare.net and enter your email to access to the class. When you register, you'll also get more free workbooks, video classes and more tools for cultivating deeper courage, compassion, and creativity in the Becoming Who You Are Library (I will never, ever share your email and you are free to unsubscribe at any time).

If you'd like to get in touch with any questions or comments, please email me at hannah@becomingwhoyouare.net. I can't always respond to every message I receive, but I do take time to read them all.

Until next time, take care.

Hannah

> "Owning our story can be hard but not nearly as difficult as spending our lives running from it."
>
> —Brené Brown, *The Gifts of Imperfection: Let Go of Who You Think You're Supposed to Be and Embrace Who You Are*

Questions for Reflection

1. *What have you learned about yourself while reading and working through the questions and practices in this book?*
2. *What are 5 to 10 things you'd like to take away from this book, even if you forget everything else?*
3. *How do you plan to nurture the connection with your*

inner mentor going forward? And how do you plan to deal with any attacks from your inner critics?

4. *Imagine you are sitting here 10 years from now, writing the present you a letter. What would you say to yourself today about life in 10 years' time? What advice or encouragement would your future self offer you of today? Make a note of these words of wisdom, put them somewhere safe, and return to them whenever you need inspiration and reassurance.*

APPENDIX

QUESTIONS FOR REFLECTION

Here you'll find all the reflective questions for each of the previous chapters of this book. Each question can stand alone, however, you might also find it helpful to go back and re-read the corresponding chapter. I suggest working through these questions one at a time, giving yourself plenty of space and time to consider each one. There is no hurry.

Part I: Introducing Your Inner Critics

Chapter 1: You Contain Multitudes

1. *Can you start to pair parts of your self-dialogue with parts of your personality? Alongside your inner critic, do you also recognize an inner child, inner mentor, and true self/Aware Ego?*
2. *Over the next week, dedicate a page in your journal, or make a note on your phone, titled "Internal Dialogue". Whenever you become conscious of a particular thought about yourself running through your head,*

make a note of it. You might also find it helpful to make time for reflection at the end of each day and note down any self-talk that's been prominent over the last 24 hours. At the end of the week, review what you've written. Do you notice any patterns in your self-talk? Are there certain phrases or messages that come up more frequently than others?

3. *How have you dealt with your inner critic so far? What has worked? And what hasn't? After reading this chapter, how do you plan to approach your inner critic from here?*
4. *If you were 5 per cent more empathic with all parts of yourself over the next week, what would you do differently?*

Chapter 2: The Many Voices of the Inner Critic

1. *Which of the inner-critic types I mention in this chapter do you recognize in your own internal dialogue? When do they most often show up? Which critic has the biggest impact on your life?*
2. *Which of the inner-critic behaviours and manifestations do you experience most frequently?*
3. *What kind of language do your inner critics use? What are their catchphrases and favourite vocabulary? Are they sarcastic? Frustrated? Spiteful? Bitter? Angry?*
4. *How does your inner critic affect your life? If you have more than one, can you link specific effects to the specific types of inner critics you identified above?*

Chapter 3: Where Do Our Inner Critics Come From?

1. *What do you consider to be your primary selves? What traits or roles are important to you? How do you want other people to see you? What do you judge other people for, and how do you consider yourself to be the opposite of that?*
2. *What do you consider to be your disowned selves? What roles, qualities or traits do you judge in other people? Are there any people you value or admire around you whom make you feel inferior? What "selves" do these people embody that you don't embody yourself?*
3. *What are some of the things your critics most often criticizes? What consequences do they warn you about? List out as many as you can think of. If you aren't sure, try thinking back over the last 24 hours and recall some less-kind thoughts that came to mind about yourself. What were they?*
4. *Who (apart from your inner critics) has said these things (or similar things) to you? Who could you imagine saying these things?*
5. *What were your conditions of worth as you were growing up and into adulthood? These might be explicit expectations, for example around getting good grades or being well-behaved. It might also include unspoken expectations and roles, for example around being the family caretaker (or the family baby), or ideas you internalized from peers and authority figures about the "proper" way to be. List as many as you can think of.*
6. *Return to the list in question 3 of things your inner critics have said to you. What do you think they might be trying to protect you from in these situations? If you look beneath their hurtful words and harsh criticism, how are they trying to help you?*

Chapter 4: Five Common Lies Your Inner Critic Tells

1. *What stories does your inner critic tell you about when you'll be good enough? What conditions does it set?*
2. *Write out a list of beliefs your inner critics currently act from. You can add to this list over the next days, weeks and months as you identify new beliefs. Then, work through each belief and ask yourself: What do I want to believe about this? What is the truth here? Replace each outdated or no-longer-relevant belief with an alternative set of beliefs you want to live by in the present.*
3. *How have your inner critics influenced your behaviour? List two or three specific examples you can think of. How do you feel reflecting on those examples now? What would you do differently if you could go back and relive those situations?*

Chapter 5: Inner Critics Need Hugs Too

1. *Keep a diary for at least the next week or month, answering the questions below at the end of each day for the 24 hours prior:*

- *What behaviours or qualities do you judge in other people? How do you feel about these behaviours or qualities within yourself?*
- *What do you hope people never learn, realize or see about you? What do you not want people to know about you?*
- *Who do you most often compare yourself to? What qualities does that person have that you would like*

more of yourself? What potential is this comparison pointing to that you're not owning in yourself?

Part II: The Inner Mentor

Chapter 6: What Is the Inner Mentor?

1. *What name resonates for you as you think about this aspect of yourself? What qualities would you like this part of yourself to have? What do you see his or her main role as? Finally, how do you imagine yourself feeling in the presence of your inner mentor? (For example, calm, held, supported, encouraged, challenged, seen, heard or whatever feels important to you.)*
2. *Look at the list of feelings you wrote in response to the last set of reflective questions. When have you felt that way, especially within yourself? What was happening at that time? Who were you with? How were you talking to yourself? What prompted that self-talk?*
3. *What messages would you like your inner mentor to reflect to you? Which of those messages feel most important? What would you most like to hear from her or him?*

Chapter 7: Inner Critic or Inner Mentor?

1. *Of the two types of motivation (motivation by fear or motivation by growth), which do you feel is more present in your life right now? How does this influence your self-talk?*
2. *What are your healthy values? If you'd like help with identifying these, you can get a free* Discover Your

Values *workbook at:* http://
bit.ly/discoveryourvalues

3. *Over the next week, make time each evening (even five minutes is enough) to check in with yourself and review any notable thoughts, feelings, reactions and decisions, from the day. Which do you think were dominated by your inner critic? And which by the inner mentor? How did the energy feel with each? Where did the feelings associated with each show up in your body? Do you notice any patterns?*

Chapter 8: Turn Up the Volume on Your Inner Mentor

1. *In which areas of your life have you been working with a fixed mindset? How has your inner critic influenced this? What would it look like to shift to a growth mindset in these areas? How would you talk to yourself if you had a growth mindset? How would you approach challenges, obstacles and successes? How would you feel differently about this area of your life?*
2. *Practise using AIR with your inner critics. Start by thinking about a recent time you experienced one or more of your critics becoming vocal. What would you have done differently, if you had used the AIR framework? How would you have responded? How would you have felt? As you develop a more mindful relationship with your inner critics, experiment with using this practice in real time.*
3. *Start a regular journaling practice, using the prompts I've shared in this chapter and return to them regularly to practise reconnecting with your inner mentor.*

Chapter 9: Mentor and Critic: A Superhero Duo

1. *In which situations are your critics most likely to appear? How do you want to respond to them in those situations? How do you think changing your response would alter how you feel about those situations? What would change in your life as a result?*
2. *In which situations do you think your critics (working alongside your inner mentor) could be most helpful in your life?*
3. *How would you like to approach these situations going forward, so you can enjoy a constructive collaboration between your inner mentor and your inner critics?*

Conclusion: Your Self-kindness Journey Starts Here

1. *What have you learned about yourself while reading and working through the questions and practices in this book?*
2. *What are 5 to 10 things you'd like to take away from this book, even if you forget everything else?*
3. *How do you plan to nurture the connection with your inner mentor going forward? And how do you plan to deal with any attacks from your inner critics?*
4. *Imagine you are sitting here 10 years from now, writing the present you a letter. What would you say to yourself today about life in 10 years' time? What advice or encouragement would your future self offer you of today? Make a note of these words of wisdom, put them somewhere safe, and return to them whenever you need inspiration and reassurance.*

RESOURCES

Cultivating a good relationship with yourself is the work of a lifetime. Below is a list of resources I've mentioned during the book that will help you continue transforming your inner critic.

Beck, Martha. *Finding Your North Star: How to Claim the Life You Were Meant to Live*. Piatkus, 2003.

Ben-Shahar, Tal. *The Pursuit of Perfect: How to Stop Chasing Perfection and Start Living a Richer, Happier Life.* McGraw Hill, 2009.

Braime, Hannah. *From Coping to Thriving: How to Turn Self-Care Into a Way of Life*. Individuate Press, 2013.

___________. *The Ultimate Guide to Journaling*. Individuate Press, 2013.

___________. "Discover Your Values," Becoming Who You Are; http://bit.ly/discoveryourvalues

___________. "How to Choose Between Coaching, Counselling and Therapy", Becoming Who You Are, November 25, 2013; https://www.becomingwhoyouare.net/choose-coaching-counselling-therapy

___________. "Be Your Own Hero", Becoming Who You Are; https://www.becomingwhoyouare.net/classes

Brown, Brené. *Rising Strong*. Vermilion, 2015.

___________. *The Gifts of Imperfection: Let Go of Who You Think You're Supposed to Be and Embrace Who You Are.* Hazelden FIRM, 2010.

___________. *Daring Greatly: How the Courage to Be Vulnerable Transforms the Way We Live, Love, Parent, and Lead*. Penguin Life, 2015.

Branden, Nathaniel. *Six Pillars of Self-Esteem.* Bantam Books, 1994.

___________. *Sentence Completion I;* http://nathanielbranden.com/sentence-completion-i

Buckley, Randi. "Healthy Boundaries for Kind People"; https://www.randibuckley.com/healthy-boundaries-for-kind-people

Chadwick, Dara. "Self-Acceptance Versus Self-Improvement", *Psychology Today,* September 11, 2009; https://www.psychologytoday.com/blog/youd-be-so-pretty-if/200909/self-acceptance-versus-self-improvement

Dweck, Carol. *Mindset: Changing the Way You Think to Fulfil Your Potential*. Robinson, 2017.

Earley, Jay. *Self-Therapy: A Step-By-Step Guide to Creating Wholeness and Healing Your Inner Child Using IFS, A New, Cutting-Edge Psychotherapy*. Pattern System Books, 2010.

Emerald, David. *The Power of TED* (*The Empowerment Dynamic)*. Polaris Publishing, 2009.

___________. www.powerofted.com

Fjelstad, Margalis. "More Questions About the Inner Critic", *Psychology Today*, 22 November, 2014; https://www.psychologytoday.com/blog/stop-caretaking-the-borderline-or-narcissist/201411/more-questions-about-the-inner-critic

Gerhardt, Sue. *Why Love Matters: How Affection Shapes a Baby's Brain*. Routledge, 2014.

Hanson, Rick. *Buddha's Brain: The Practical Neuroscience of Happiness, Love, and Wisdom*. New Harbinger, 2009.

Katherine, Anne. *Boundaries Where You End and I Begin: How to Recognize and Set Healthy Boundaries*. Touchstone, 2001.

___________. *Where to Draw the Line: How to Set Healthy Boundaries Every Day*. Simon and Schuster, 2000.

Lee Cori, Jasmin. *The Emotionally Absent Mother: A Guide to*

Self-Healing and Getting the Love You Missed. The Experiment, LLC, 2010.

Mohr, Tara. *Playing Big: A Practical Guide for Brilliant Women Like You*. Arrow, 2015.

Neff, Kristen. *Self-Compassion: Stop Beating Yourself Up and Leave Insecurity Behind*. Yellow Kite, 2011.

___________. "Why We Need to Have Compassion for Our Inner Critic", Self-Compassion; http://self-compassion.org/why-we-need-to-have-compassion-for-our-inner-critic

Petherick, Sas and Buckley, Randi, "Episode 13: Healthy, Kind Boundaries for the Holidays", Courage and Spice podcast, November 30, 2017; http://courageandspice.com/episode-13-healthy-kind-boundaries-holidays/

Rogers, Carl. *On Becoming A Person: A Therapist's View of Psychotherapy*. Robinson, 2004.

Rubin, Gretchen. *The Happiness Project: Or, Why I Spent a Year Trying to Sing in the Morning, Clean My Closets, Fight Right, Read Aristotle, and Generally Have More Fun*. Harper, 2011.

Meg Selig, "Manage Emotional Pain with RAINS", *Psychology Today*, February 06, 2012; https://www.psychologytoday.com/blog/changepower/201202/manage-emotional-pains-rains

Simon, Tami (ed.), *The Self-Acceptance Project: How to Be Kind and Compassionate Towards Yourself in Any Situation.* Sounds True, 2016.

Stone, Hal & Sidra. *Embracing Your Inner Critic: Turning Self-Criticism Into a Creative Asset*. Bravo Ltd, 1993.

ALSO BY HANNAH BRAIME

From Coping to Thriving: How to Turn Self-Care Into a Way of Life

***From Coping to Thriving* is a comprehensive guide to making self-care part of your everyday life.** With a balance between practical suggestions, coaching-style questions and psychological groundwork, this book is designed to give you the self-knowledge and awareness you need to start making self-care an integral part of your life. Not only does *From Coping to Thriving* contain hundreds of useful self-care tips and ideas, it will also take you deeper into related topics like habit-formation, coping strategies, dealing with resistance to self-care and more.

The Ultimate Guide to Journaling

In *The Ultimate Guide to Journaling*, you'll find the tips, inspiration and prompts you need to start and maintain a journaling practice for DIY self-discovery. This clear and concise handbook shares everything you need to know to deepen your relationship with yourself using this powerful personal development tool. Covering foundational topics like how to journal, which tools to use, and how to make it a regular habit, as well as over 30 different journaling techniques and many more prompts, *The Ultimate Guide to Journaling* will help you keep your practice flowing for years to come.

The Year of You: 365 Journal Writing Prompts for Creative Self-Discovery

Are you ready to go on a journey? ***The Year of You* is an invitation to discover more about yourself, become more conscious about what you want, and create a rich and**

fulfilling life through one journaling prompt a day. This book provides you with 365 structured journaling prompts to explore the most important areas of your life, from identity, health, and relationships, to money, career, and the future. Whether you're new to journaling or have enjoyed a reflective writing practice for some time, this book provides a wealth of inspiration that will deepen your understanding and awareness of what makes you who you are.

ACKNOWLEDGMENTS

A huge thank you to everyone who collaborated on and contributed to this book, whether they were directly aware of it or not.

Thank you to everyone who reads Becoming Who You Are and especially those who took the time to give their feedback on the title and cover for this book. Extra special thanks to Sherrill, Sebastian, Tom, Cynthia, Lucy, Mary-olin, Mallory, Angie, Anita, plus everyone else who shared their personal experiences with self-kindness and their inner critics. Thank you also to Stephanie Murphy for narrating the audiobook version and doing an amazing job - as always!

Thank you to all the psychologists, authors, and coaches whose ideas and quotes I have shared in this book. Thanks especially to David Emerald and Jay Earley for all the valuable work they do in the world and for giving me permission to share their frameworks in this book. Thank you also to Sandy Draper for her edits.

Finally, thank you to my two favourite people: Jake for his support and feedback and to Freya for her joie de vivre and for being my biggest teacher. I feel lucky every day to have you both in my life.

ABOUT THE AUTHOR

Hannah Braime is a creative life coach and author who writes about self-care, journaling and creativity. She is the author of four books, including *From Coping to Thriving: How to Turn Self-Care Into a Way of Life* and *The Year of You: 365 Journal-Writing Prompts for Creative Self-Discovery.* She also shares inspiring psychology-based articles and resources on creating a full and meaningful life with greater courage, compassion and creativity at http://www.becomingwhoyouare.net.

Made in the USA
Middletown, DE
12 March 2020

86267513R00116